THOMAS JEFFERSON

by Nancy Skarmeas

IDEALS PUBLICATIONS INCORPORATED

NASHVILLE, TENNESSEE

ISBN 0-8249-4086-5

Printed and bound in the U.S.A. by R. R. Donnelley & Sons, Roanoke, Virginia.

Library of Congress Cataloging-in-Publication Data

Thomas Jefferson.
     p. cm. -- (Great Americans)
   Includes bibliographical references and index.
   ISBN 0-8249-4086-5
   1. Jefferson, Thomas, 1743–1826. 2. Presidents--United
States--Biography. 3. Jefferson, Thomas, 1743–1826--Pictorial
works. 4. Jefferson, Thomas, 1743–1826--Quotations. I. Jefferson,
Thomas, 1743–1826. II. Ideals Publications Incorporated. III.
Series: Great Americans (Nashville, Tenn.)
   E332 .T42 1998
   973.4'6'092--dc21
     [B]   98-28054
                                                  CIP

First Edition
10 8 6 4 2 1 3 5 7 9

The paper used in this publication meets the minimum requirements of American National Standard for Information Sciences—Permanence of Paper for Printed Library Materials, ANSI Z39,48-1984.

Published by Ideals Publications Incorporated
535 Metroplex Drive, Suite 250
Nashville, Tennessee 37211

Art on cover:
Portrait of Thomas Jefferson by Rembrandt Peale,
The White House Historical Association.

Engraving of Jefferson on half-title page and cover:
photo Archive Photos.
Art on title page:
Delegates of Congress in Philadelphia
Sign the U.S. Declaration of Independence
Drafted by Thomas Jefferson
John Trumbull, 1756–1843
Yale University, New Haven CT/A.K.G., Berlin/SuperStock.
Art on page 82:
Portrait of Thomas Jefferson by Gilbert Stuart. National Portrait Gallery, Smithsonian Institution; gift of the Regents of the Smithsonian Institution, the Thomas Jefferson Memorial Foundation, and the Enid and Crosby Kemper Foundation; owned jointly with Monticello.

We are deeply indebted to Dr. Peter Onuf, Thomas Jefferson Memorial Foundation Professor of History at the University of Virginia, for his invaluable assistance in verifying the historical accuracy of the manuscript.

We also extend our heartfelt appreciation to Whitney Espich, Communications Officer of the Thomas Jefferson Memorial Foundation, for providing many of the photographs in the book and for her generosity in giving her time and expertise to review the book.

Publisher and Editor: Patricia A. Pingry
Associate Editor: Michelle Prater Burke
Designer: Eve DeGrie
Copy Editor: Kristi Richardson
Editorial Assistant: Christine Landry

ACKNOWLEDGMENTS

An excerpted letter reprinted from THE FAMILY LETTERS OF THOMAS JEFFERSON edited by Edwin Morris Betts and James Adam Bear Jr., by permission of the University of Missouri Press. Copyright © 1966 by the Curators of the University of Missouri. Excerpts reprinted by permission of Louisiana State University Press from IN PURSUIT OF REASON: THE LIFE OF THOMAS JEFFERSON, by Noble E. Cunningham, Jr. Copyright © 1987 by Louisiana State University Press. An excerpt from LEWIS & CLARK by Dayton Duncan, copyright © 1997 by the American Lives Film Project, Inc. Reprinted by permission of Alfred A. Knopf, Inc. Excerpts from "Jefferson as a Civil Libertarian" in CONSTITUTIONAL OPINIONS: ASPECTS OF THE BILL OF RIGHTS by Leonard W. Levy. Copyright © 1986 by the author; reprinted with permission. An excerpt from THE AMERICAN POLITICAL TRADITION by Richard Hofstadter. Copyright © 1949 by Alfred A. Knopf, Inc. and renewed 1976 by Beatrice Hofstadter. Reprinted by permission of the publisher. Excerpts from JEFFERSON HIMSELF, edited by Bernard Mayo. Copyright © 1942, renewed 1970 by Bernard Mayo. Reprinted by permission of Houghton Mifflin Company. All rights reserved. Excerpts from JEFFERSON AND THE RIGHTS OF MAN by Dumas Malone. Copyright © 1951, 1979 by Dumas Malone. Reprinted by permission of Little, Brown and Company. Excerpts from JEFFERSON THE VIRGINIAN by Dumas Malone. Copyright © 1948, 1976 by Dumas Malone. Reprinted by permission of Little, Brown and Company. Excerpts from JEFFERSON AND MONTICELLO by John McLaughlin. Copyright © 1988 by John McLaughlin. Reprinted by permission of Henry Holt and Company. Excerpts by Gordon S. Wood and Michael Lienesch from JEFFERSONIAN LEGACIES, edited by Peter S. Onuf. Copyright © 1993 by the Rector and Visitors of the University of Virginia. Reprinted with permission of the University Press of Virginia. Excerpts from THOMAS JEFFERSON AND THE NEW NATION: A BIOGRAPHY by Merrill D. Peterson. Copyright © 1970 by Oxford University Press, Inc. Used by permission of Oxford University Press, Inc.

Contents

PREFACE

Thomas Jefferson was born in central Virginia in 1743, on the edge of the American frontier and at the cusp of the American Revolution. He was raised to live the conventional and comfortable life of a wealthy Virginia planter, but his character and intellect marked him as entirely unconventional. Inspired by the words of the great English philosophers of the Enlightenment, Jefferson came of age with a passionate belief in the natural rights of each individual and an unfailing conviction that man had the power to improve and even perfect his societies. He was also blessed with a particular gift for written expression and an insatiable curiosity about the world around him. The insular and static world of Virginia plantation society could not hold Thomas Jefferson; he was destined to leave his mark upon his nation and the world.

Jefferson's catalogue of achievements has few equals in American history. A two-term president, Jefferson was also elected vice president and governor of Virginia. In the early years of American independence, he served as minister to France, and George Washington appointed him the nation's first secretary of state. With his pen, Jefferson gave the world the Declaration of Independence and the Virginia Act for Establishing Religious Freedom. He was a patriot, an architect, a scholar, a philosopher, and a farmer; and his intellectual curiosity knew no bounds. Without ever venturing west of Virginia's mountains, he was an explorer whose vision opened the American continent to future generations of settlers and citizens. And as the American nation grew and tested its wings, Jefferson emerged as a voice of reason, zealously guarding against too great an exertion of power by the federal government while at the same time understanding the responsibility of that federal government to lead and protect the people.

More than a century and a half after his death, Jefferson is readily invoked by those on opposing sides of nearly every political battle in American life. In the eyes of many Americans, Jefferson is one of the venerable Founding Fathers whose words and intentions stand immutable. But for every American ready to lionize Jefferson, there is another ready to malign him. Entire volumes have been devoted to his character flaws. Most significantly, the troubling contradiction of his slaveholding is con-

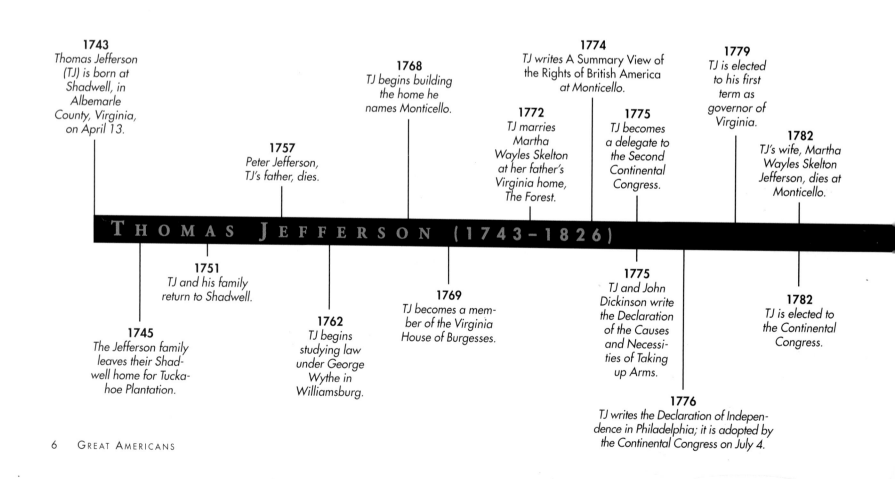

1743
Thomas Jefferson (TJ) is born at Shadwell, in Albemarle County, Virginia, on April 13.

1757
Peter Jefferson, TJ's father, dies.

1768
TJ begins building the home he names Monticello.

1774
TJ writes A Summary View of the Rights of British America at Monticello.

1772
TJ marries Martha Wayles Skelton at her father's Virginia home, The Forest.

1775
TJ becomes a delegate to the Second Continental Congress.

1779
TJ is elected to his first term as governor of Virginia.

1782
TJ's wife, Martha Wayles Skelton Jefferson, dies at Monticello.

THOMAS JEFFERSON (1743–1826)

1751
TJ and his family return to Shadwell.

1745
The Jefferson family leaves their Shadwell home for Tuckahoe Plantation.

1762
TJ begins studying law under George Wythe in Williamsburg.

1769
TJ becomes a member of the Virginia House of Burgesses.

1775
TJ and John Dickinson write the Declaration of the Causes and Necessities of Taking up Arms.

1776
TJ writes the Declaration of Independence in Philadelphia; it is adopted by the Continental Congress on July 4.

1782
TJ is elected to the Continental Congress.

tinuously in debate; whereas Jefferson spent his life writing and speaking about the natural rights of man, he neither freed his slaves in his lifetime nor worked with true commitment toward the end of slavery in the United States.

But Jefferson's legacy must not be undermined by character flaws or contradictions, for it was ideas that made him great—ideas much larger than any single individual, including himself. "Nothing then is unchangeable," Jefferson wrote in the last years of his life, "but the inherent and unalienable rights of man." This belief was Jefferson's gift to the world. He did not invent the concept of natural rights, but he was its most eloquent and devoted spokesman; and it was Jefferson, more than any other individual, who helped this idea find permanent expression in the founding of the American nation.

An optimist to the end of his days, Jefferson would likely be heartened by both the wide ideological range of his supporters and by the criticism heaped upon him by those intent upon reshaping the country and reinterpreting its history. The earth, he was fond of saying, belongs to the living. By this he meant that each generation has the power—and the responsibility—to think for itself. Leaders come and go, Jefferson knew, and he never expected any special reverence after his passing. What he

did hope was that the ideals upon which the nation had been founded would remain foremost in the minds of the American people. Any individual who studies Jefferson's life, who criticizes his character or his actions, who enlightens the present through study of this great life of the past, is a living affirmation of the belief that sustained Jefferson in his final days. "I shall not die," he wrote to his friend John Adams in his last years, "without a hope that light and liberty are on steady advance."

In the pages that follow is a portrait of Thomas Jefferson, drawn from his own words, the observations of those who knew him, the interpretations of scholars and historians, and a collection of paintings, sketches, and photographs of the people and places in Jefferson's life. The result is not a traditional or comprehensive biography, but rather an eclectic collection meant to bring to light both the man and the revolutionary era in which he lived. We present this volume with the firm belief that Thomas Jefferson was among the greatest of Americans, and that nothing was more fundamental to our nation's birth, or is more vital to its continued growth and well-being, than his passionate commitment to the natural, inalienable rights of each and every citizen.

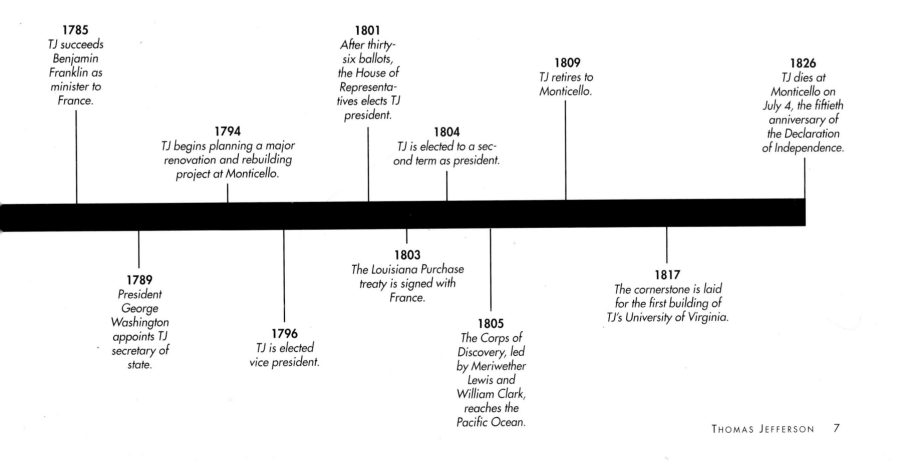

1785
TJ succeeds Benjamin Franklin as minister to France.

1794
TJ begins planning a major renovation and rebuilding project at Monticello.

1801
After thirty-six ballots, the House of Representatives elects TJ president.

1804
TJ is elected to a second term as president.

1809
TJ retires to Monticello.

1826
TJ dies at Monticello on July 4, the fiftieth anniversary of the Declaration of Independence.

1789
President George Washington appoints TJ secretary of state.

1796
TJ is elected vice president.

1803
The Louisiana Purchase treaty is signed with France.

1805
The Corps of Discovery, led by Meriwether Lewis and William Clark, reaches the Pacific Ocean.

1817
The cornerstone is laid for the first building of TJ's University of Virginia.

THE VIRGINIAN
1743–1768

Thomas Jefferson
A Philosopher a Patriote and a Friend
Dessiné par son Ami Tadée Kosciuszko
Et Gravé par Mr. Sokolnicki

Thomas Jefferson was born in 1743 on the edge of the American frontier, in a central Virginia farmhouse his parents called Shadwell. To the southeast lay the capital city of Williamsburg, the center of culture and commerce in the colony; to the west, the Blue Ridge Mountains, gateway to the vast and uncharted western lands of the continent. Jefferson would grow to exert a powerful influence on both these worlds, but neither the frontier nor the city would ever truly claim him. Throughout a long and accomplished life, Jefferson would remain loyal to the region of his birth, and he would end his days only miles from where he began them, in the midst of the hills and rivers of central Virginia.

At left, a portrait of Thomas Jefferson by Thaddeus Kosciuszko, The Pierpont Morgan Library/Art Resource, NY. At right, a modern view of Williamsburg, Virginia. Photo SuperStock.

BORN IN THE PROVINCE OF VIRGINIA

FROM *JEFFERSON THE VIRGINIAN*, BY DUMAS MALONE

1743

Thomas Jefferson (TJ) is born at Shadwell, in Albemarle County, Virginia, on April 13.

1745–46

The Jefferson family leaves their Shadwell home for Tuckahoe Plantation, where TJ's father takes on the role of guardian to the children of his deceased friend William Randolph.

1748

TJ begins his formal education in a schoolhouse on Tuckahoe Plantation.

1749

British Parliament legalizes slavery in the American colonies.

1749

King George II of England charters the Ohio Company to settle land in the upper Ohio River valley.

1751

TJ and his family return to Shadwell.

1751

James Madison is born in Port Conway, Virginia.

1751

English Parliament passes the Currency Act, which forbids the colonies of New England from issuing their own money.

1752

Benjamin Franklin conducts an experiment with a kite and a key to prove that lightening is the result of electrical charges.

1753

A ship leaves Philadelphia to explore Hudson's Straits in search of the Northwest Passage across the continent.

Very little is known of Jefferson's childhood; no letters survive from the era, and most family documents were destroyed by fire in 1770. Jefferson himself revealed little of his early life in his own voluminous writings. The most significant single event from his youth appears to have been the death of his father, Peter Jefferson, in 1757. The most powerful influence on his development, as biographer Dumas Malone describes here, was undoubtedly the land and society of his native Virginia.

Thomas Jefferson was born in a simple wooden house in what is now Albemarle County, Virginia. At that time the district was in the County of Goochland, and Virginia was a province of King George II of Great Britain. By the calendar then in effect the birthday was April 2, 1743, but according to the New Style, which was adopted when Jefferson was still a boy, it was April 13, and thus it has been celebrated through the years. This was a delicious season, for the air of the Virginia Piedmont is soft in April, the dogwood soon opens in the woods, and the wild honeysuckle begins to bloom. The house has long since vanished, but the site is marked and anybody who goes there now can see that it was well chosen. To the southward it overlooks the Rivanna River, often referred to then as the North River or North Branch of the James. This is now a muddy and unimpressive stream but it was once purer. The prospect to the west is finer, for on any clear day the distant Blue Ridge can be seen through a gap in the Southwest Mountains.

The place was called Shadwell. Peter Jefferson, who owned it, had named it for the parish in London where his wife, Jane Randolph, had been christened twenty-three years before. The setting did not suggest the Thames Basin or Hanoverian England, however. This was not a rainy but generally a sunny land, and it had no antiquity or mellowness, for as a seat of settlement it was almost wholly new. The hardwood forests which covered the bottom lands and steep hillsides were broken by only a few clearings where the red soil glowed, and the first wails of this newborn infant could have been echoed by the howling of the wolves. The earliest surroundings of this natural philosopher were beautiful but they were wild. Jefferson was born on the fringe of western settlement, and some will say that he thus became a child of the American frontier.

No influence upon him was more abiding than that of Nature, and throughout life he deeply loved this region of wooded hills and lavender-tinted mountains. But Shadwell was not the home of his earliest memories. When he was two or three years old he was taken from it to Tuckahoe on the James, to an older and better house in a more thickly settled district. At that time no parts of Virginia were thickly settled; with a few exceptions the entire Province was a vast forest. Tobacco plantations and their seats were strung loosely along the rivers, but to all European observers the clearings seemed small and the country looked uninhabited. The vastness of this physical setting was not lost on Thomas Jefferson; it was reflected in the largeness of his mind. Furthermore, this society as a whole was closer to the frontier than later generations might at first realize. But Jefferson was in Albemarle only intermittently during his boyhood, and he knew the region best after the fringe of settlement had stretched well beyond it. He was used to sparsely settled country, but he did not know the frontier by experience; and though he was always aware of the wilderness, he was not in the physical sense an explorer. . . .

The most important early fact about Thomas Jefferson is not that he appeared on the edge of settlement but that he was born in the Province of Virginia and that, from his first days, he was numbered among its gentry. He was not born to physical hardship as Abraham Lincoln was; he did not know town life from boyhood as Benjamin Franklin did; in the ordinary meaning of the term he was no self-made man. He grew up in the generous society which had been created in a new country and a warm climate by a group of planters, cultivating tobacco and relying upon slave labor. From his earliest memories his financial position was assured, and the best educational opportunities which the Colony afforded were later available to him.

Jefferson's lifelong love of the landscape of his native state would find its most passionate expression in his devotion to Monticello, the home he designed and built in the hills of central Virginia, not far from his birthplace. Above all else, it was the view of the surrounding land that made Jefferson choose a mountain-top site for Monticello. His own words describe his rapture at the feeling of standing and looking out at the landscape below: "And our own dear Monticello, where has nature spread so rich a mantle under the eye? Mountains, forests, rocks, rivers. With what majesty do we ride above the storms! How sublime to look down into the workhouse of nature, to see her clouds, hail, snow, rain, thunder, all fabricated at our feet! And the glorious Sun, when rising as if out of distant water, just gliding the tops of the mountains, and giving life to all nature!" Above, artist Jane Braddick Peticolas's watercolor rendering of the view from Monticello in 1825. Visible in the distance are the buildings of the University of Virginia, the project of Jefferson's retirement years. Peticolas was one of the few artists to paint or draw Monticello and its views during Jefferson's lifetime. Watercolor the Thomas Jefferson Memorial Foundation.

The tradition in my father's family was, that their ancestor came to this country from Wales, and from near the mountain of Snowdon, the highest in Great Britain. . . . The first particular information I have of any ancestor was of my grandfather, who lived at the place in Chesterfield called Ozborne's, and owned the lands afterwards the glebe of the parish. He had three sons; Thomas who died young, Field who settled on the waters of Roanoke and left numerous descendants, and Peter, my father, who settled on the lands I still own, called Shadwell, adjoining my present residence. He was born on February 29, 1707–8, and intermarried 1739, with Jane Randolph, of the age of 19, daughter of Isham Randolph, one of the seven sons of that name and family, settled at Dungeoness in Goochland. They trace their pedigree far back in England and Scotland, to which let every one ascribe the faith and merit he chooses.

My father's education had been quite neglected; but being of a strong mind, sound judgment, and eager after information, he read much and improved himself, insomuch that he was chosen, with Joshua Fry, Professor of Mathematics in William and Mary college, to continue the boundary line between Virginia and North Carolina . . . and was afterwards employed with the same Mr. Fry, to make the first map of Virginia which had ever been made. . . . He died, August 17th, 1757, leaving my mother a widow who lived until 1776, with six daughters and two sons, myself the elder. . . .

He placed me at the English school at five years of age; and at the Latin at nine, where I continued until his death. My teacher, Mr. Douglas, a clergyman from Scotland, with the rudiments of the Latin and Greek languages, taught me the French; and on the death of my father, I went to the Reverend Mr. Maury, a correct classical scholar, with whom I continued two years; and then, to wit, in the spring of 1760, went to William and Mary college, where I continued two years.

Thomas Jefferson, from his Autobiography

A WILLIAMSBURG EDUCATION

FROM *THOMAS JEFFERSON AND THE NEW NATION*, BY MERRILL D. PETERSON

1754

The first battle of the French and Indian War is fought; George Washington commands the colonial forces.

1754

Benjamin Franklin leads a failed attempt to unite the British colonies in America under a single ruler.

1754

John Woolman writes Some Considerations on the Keeping of Negroes, in which he urges fellow Quakers to free their slaves.

1756

A direct stagecoach route between New York City and Philadelphia is opened.

1757

Peter Jefferson, TJ's father, dies.

1757

Alexander Hamilton is born in the West Indies in January.

1758

The French and Indian War continues; the British drive the French from Fort Dusquesne and rename it Pittsburgh.

1758

James Monroe is born in Westmoreland County, Virginia.

1760

TJ enrolls at The College of William and Mary in Williamsburg, Virginia.

1760

The French surrender the city of Montreal to British forces.

At the age of seventeen, Jefferson traveled to Williamsburg to begin his studies at The College of William and Mary. After a first year in which he found himself often distracted by the excitement and variety of town life, Jefferson settled in to become one of William and Mary's most committed students. Despite his youth, he was accepted into the society of the best minds in Williamsburg; these men fanned the flames of his natural intellectual curiosity and introduced him to the rational and scientific thinking of the Enlightenment.

This youth of seventeen who came down from the hills to Williamsburg in 1760 had taken on the physical characteristics so commonly ascribed to him in later years. He was tall and lanky, with large hands and feet, and seemed to be growing right out of his clothes. As straight and strong as a gun barrel, he had the sinewy, broad-shouldered vigor of his father. His tousled hair was of a reddish color, his eyes light and hazel, his face ruddy and freckled. His head, like his body, was spare of flesh. Lips thin and compressed suggested a mind in thought, while the angular nose and projecting chin added forcefulness to a countenance otherwise mild. He gave the appearance of the fresh country lad he was, rather more awkward than graceful, and by no stretch could he be considered handsome or polished at this stage. But he was bright, amiable, eager, and full of bounce, which more than compensated for any deficiency in looks.

Williamsburg was a new scene. To begin with it was a town, that rarity in Virginia young Jefferson had not known before. It was also the provincial capital, seat of empire in the New World, about as little felt in Albemarle as His Majesty's government across the ocean, but, nevertheless, the hub of Virginia politics, society, and culture. Close to 1500 people lived in the town. During "publick times" in the spring and fall, however, when the General Court and the House of Burgesses were in session, the population doubled. Between the College at one end and the Capitol at the other stretched a mile-long thoroughfare, Duke of Gloucester Street, through which coursed a colorful parade of humanity. In the years ahead Jefferson came to know every feature of this artery and its tributaries—the Bruton Church where he sometimes worshiped, the Raleigh Tavern where he danced and flirted and on occasion minded weighty affairs of state, the shops he patronized, the houses he visited. . . . In the surrounding country were the princely estates of tidewater aristocrats who wielded power at Williamsburg. Sons of several of these patrician families—Harrisons, Burwells, Pages, and others—were among Jefferson's classmates at college, and he easily made his way into their society, so much grander than anything he had known in the upcountry.

Jefferson lived and studied for two years in the College. Chartered by the Crown in 1693, receiving its name from the reigning sovereigns, and floated on the profits of Virginia lands and tobacco, the College had a distinctive public character. It had a religious character too, being founded in part to provide ministers for the established Church of England and being under the control of the Church; but unlike the sister colleges to the north—more emphatically ecclesiastical in character—William and Mary failed miserably in this object. Few of the planters' sons who went there chose a ministerial career, with the result that the College was constantly at war with itself, torn between the brazen secularism of the community it served and its clerical mission. The College had grown into a miscellaneous assortment of schools: a preparatory or grammar school presided over by a master; an Indian school, the Brafferton, intended to Christianize the natives, also with a single master; the philosophy school, which was the equivalent of a liberal arts college, with two professors; and the divinity school, similarly staffed. Not more than a hundred students were enrolled in all the schools. Over the whole sat a president, who also usually occupied the position of commissary, as agent of the Bishop of London in the colony, and the pulpit of Bruton Church, and who at the time of Jefferson's entrance into the College was a notorious drunkard. Jefferson, of course, enrolled in the philosophy school where "systems of logick, physicks, ethicks and mathematicks" were dispensed by the two professors.

"It was my great good fortune, and what probably fixed the destinies of my life," Jefferson wrote in his autobiography, "that Dr. William Small of Scotland, was then Professor of Mathematics, a man profound in most of the useful branches of science, with a happy talent of communication, correct and gentlemanly manners, and an enlarged and liberal mind. He, most happily for me, became soon attached to me, and made me his daily companion when not engaged in the school; and from his conversation I got my first views of the expansion of science, and of the system of things in which we are placed." This gentleman, the single non-clergyman on the faculty, had only recently come to the College, and he remained but six years. Judging by his later friendship, after his return to England, with James Watt, Erasmus Darwin, and others of the Birmingham scientific circle, Small was a man of talents not far below the mark assigned to him by his favorite student. He had been swept up in the enlightened thought of the age. His teaching was rational and scientific rather than religious and didactic; and he gave this cast to Jefferson's mind. He was, in fact, the first truly enlightened or scientific man the young student had encountered.

In his Autobiography, Jefferson described the profound influence that his teachers at William and Mary had on him. Dr. William Small, Jefferson's professor of mathematics, introduced him to George Wythe, under whom he would later study law, and also to Virginia's Governor Fauquier. The young student and these three distinguished men met often at the Governor's Palace, pictured at right, and their dinner conversations served as a second college for young Jefferson as he developed and refined the principles that would guide him throughout his life. Photo SuperStock.

The eighteenth-century Enlightenment represented the pushing back [of] the boundaries of darkness and what was called Gothic barbarism and the spreading of light and knowledge. This struggle occurred on many fronts. Some saw the central battle taking place in natural science and in the increasing understanding of nature. Some saw it occurring mostly in religion with the tempering of enthusiasm and the elimination of superstition. Others saw it taking place mainly in politics—in driving back the forces of tyranny and in the creating of new free governments. Still others saw it in the spread of civility and refinement and in the increase in the small, seemingly insignificant ways that life was being made easier, politer, more comfortable, and more enjoyable for more and more people. In one way or another all of these Enlightenment activities involved the imposition of order and reason on the world. To contemplate aesthetically an ordered universe and to know the best that was thought and said in the world—that was enlightenment.

Jefferson participated fully in all these aspects of the eighteenth-century Enlightenment. He was probably the American revolutionary leader most taken with the age's liberal prescriptions for enlightenment, gentility, and refinement. He was the son of a wealthy but uneducated and ungenteel planter from western Virginia and the first of his father's family to go to college. Like many of the Revolutionary leaders who were also the first of their family to acquire a liberal arts education in college, he wanted a society led by an aristocracy of talent and taste. For too long men had been judged by who their fathers were or whom they had married. In a new enlightened republican society they would be judged by merit and virtue and taste alone.

Gordon S. Wood, from "The Trials and Tribulations of Thomas Jefferson"

MONTICELLO'S BEGINNINGS

FROM *JEFFERSON AND MONTICELLO*, BY JACK MCLAUGHLIN

1760

George III becomes king of England.

1760

A census measures the colonial population at 1,600,000.

1762

TJ begins studying law under George Wythe in Williamsburg.

1763

The Treaty of Paris ends the French and Indian War.

1765

British Parliament passes the Stamp Act on March 22, taxing newspapers, legal documents, and pamphlets in the colonies.

1765

The Quartering Act becomes law, requiring colonists to house British troops on command.

1765

The Stamp Act Congress is convened in New York City in opposition to the taxation imposed by the Stamp Act.

1766

Great Britain repeals the Stamp Act.

1767

John Quincy Adams, son of John Adams, is born in Braintree, Massachusetts.

1767

The Townshend Revenue Acts of the British Parliament require colonists to pay a duty on tea, glass, paint, oil, lead, and paper.

1767

TJ begins practicing law in Williamsburg.

1768

TJ begins building the home he names Monticello.

Jefferson began dreaming of building a house of his own when he was a student in Williamsburg. The site he chose was a small mountaintop one mile from Charlottesville, on property he had inherited from his father. Jefferson began building in 1768, and in 1770 he moved into the one-room cottage that would one day grow into Monticello. From its first conception in the mind of the idealistic young Jefferson, Monticello was destined to be no ordinary home.

Thomas Jefferson was in his twenty-fifth year when he began leveling the top of a small mountain with the intention of building one of the handsomest houses in his part of Virginia. The mountain was the legacy of his father, land that Peter Jefferson had amassed during a lifetime of real estate acquisition. When he died in 1757, the elder Jefferson owned approximately 7,500 acres, mostly in Albemarle, a county that leaned against the Blue Ridge mountains to the west and bordered the James River on the south. The Jefferson lands lay for the most part around the Rivanna River, a tributary that flowed southeast, past Charlottesville, and emptied into the James.

The rivers of Virginia were the commercial arteries that joined the interior counties of the Piedmont to the Tidewater, the Chesapeake, and the world. . . . Land travel by wagon, carriage, or horseback was hazardous, painful, and slow; during bad weather, it was often impossible. The great rivers of Virginia, on the other hand—the Potomac, Rappahannock, York, and James—allowed the colony's chief commercial product, tobacco, to be transported with relative ease from inland to the shipping ports of the Chesapeake. It was along these rivers that the early plantations had been carved from primeval forests, and it was at the river's edge that the great manor houses of Virginia were raised. Building next to the river was an obvious choice: the river was not only a roadway for commerce and supply, it also provided convenience for visiting neighboring plantations by small boat. There was an ample water supply readily at hand, and by clearing the land from house to river, a magnificent vista of lawn, garden, and water could be had.

In spite of all these advantages young Jefferson ignored the banks of the Rivanna River as the site for his house and chose instead the top of a nearby 867-foot mountain. In doing so, he defied conventional wisdom to the point where many of his friends and neighbors must have thought him mad. By building on top of a mountain, he not only forfeited the economic benefits and practical conveniences of a riverside location, but took on a formidable set of obstacles as well. He had to construct roads to the building site through dense, virgin forests; materials had to be hauled for considerable distances up steep inclines over poor roadbeds; and there was little water atop the mountain. Clearly then, there was only one overriding consideration that prevailed against common sense in his choice of a building location, and that was the view. . . . As any modern visitor on a clear day can verify, the view is spectacular. As a young man, Jefferson frequently climbed to the top of his mountains to enjoy that view. During the five years he studied law in Williamsburg he usually spent the summer months at his ancestral home, Shadwell, located at the foot of his "little mountain." (He was learning Italian at the time he named it Monticello.) He would study from daybreak until late afternoon, at which time he would take a gallop on horseback, and then hike to the top of his mountain to contemplate the vista, and perhaps his future plans for building a house there.

Throughout his life Jefferson had a deep and abiding love of the Virginia land and its beauties, particularly for what eighteenth-century intellectuals were fond of characterizing as "the sublime." As a counterweight to the rationality of a neoclassical age, a number of writers . . . seized upon the idea that we can be transported to moments of ecstasy by the emotions of terror, horror, and fear. These emotions are experienced most profoundly by violent manifestations of nature—tempests, raging seas, cataracts, forest fires, untamed rivers, and craggy mountains. In the eighteenth century, for example, the Alps were discovered as objects of sublime beauty rather than mere natural obstacles. Indeed, heights of every kind were admired for their vertiginous euphorias and as lofty balconies where one could view the drama enacted upon nature's stage. . . .

By deciding to build upon a mountaintop instead of at the riverside young Jefferson made an aesthetic decision over a practical one. In this first significant choice in his building program he established a pattern that was to prevail throughout a lifetime of construction. Visitors today are captivated by the practical conveniences of Monticello: the dumbwaiter, the indoor privy, the double doors that swing in unison, the cannonball clock and its ladder, the revolving table in his bedroom, the all-weather passageways from house to dependencies. These are the domestic practicalities that were in conflict with abstract aesthetic decisions in a continuing struggle throughout Jefferson's architectural career. His design style was to choose what was often an impractical but aesthetically satisfying architectural motif, and then modify it to make the space as comfortable and livable as possible. . . . So it was in deciding to build upon the top of a mountain. The site was sublime, and there he would pitch his tent, come hail or no water.

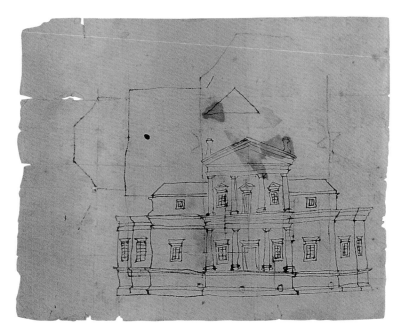

"Architecture is my delight," Jefferson once wrote, "and putting up, and pulling down, one of my favorite amusements." At left, one of Jefferson's earliest visions of Monticello, a rough ink elevation. When Jefferson first took up residence at Monticello, it was a simple, one-room cottage. He wrote of his new home in a letter to friend James Ogilvie in February of 1771: "I have lately removed to the mountain. . . . I have here but one room which . . . serves me for parlour for kitchen and hall. I may add, for bedchamber and study too. My friends sometimes take a temperate dinner with me and then retire to look for beds elsewhere. I have hopes however of getting more elbow room this summer." Sketch the Thomas Jefferson Memorial Foundation.

The Character of the Man

FROM *Thomas Jefferson and the New Nation*, BY Merrill D. Peterson

Jefferson called Sir Isaac Newton, John Locke, and Sir Francis Bacon a "trinity of the three greatest men the world had ever produced." These Englishmen, whose work in science and philosophy laid the groundwork for the Enlightenment, inspired Jefferson's passionate belief in the perfectibility of society and the natural rights of man. He eventually commissioned three portraits—one of each man—and hung them together in the parlor at Monticello. Above, a portrait of Sir Francis Bacon by an unknown artist. National Portrait Gallery, London/SuperStock. Opposite right, portrait of Sir Isaac Newton by John Vanderbank. National Portrait Gallery, London/SuperStock.

Jefferson began practicing law in 1767. Soon thereafter, as was the custom for educated landholders in Virginia, he ran for a seat in the House of Burgesses. Jefferson believed he was merely fulfilling a public duty, but circumstances and the nature of his character would combine to turn his civic duty into a life's calling and place him at the forefront of a revolution.

What manner of man was this thirty-year-old Virginian about to step to the center of the Revolutionary stage? Certain dominant traits of mind and character had formed a personal style destined to have profound public effects. While no complete accounting is possible at this point, before he was really known to history, some of the controlling features of his personality might be discerned.

One is struck, first of all, by the young Jefferson's intellectuality. He was pre-eminently a student, strenuous in the pursuit of knowledge. His mental discipline, his appetite for books, his omnivorous curiosity, all marked the trait. He approached the world through his understanding rather than his feelings. It would be misleading to call him bookish, especially if that adjective is meant to suggest the pedant or the closeted philosopher, for he was neither of these; yet, far more than most men, he was dependent on books and inclined to take his knowledge from them rather than from direct acquaintance. As a result, his understanding spanned an immense field but spanned much of it at second- or third-hand, which gave a certain airiness to his traffic with reality. He gained a vantage point above or outside of things-as-they-are—the hard crust of history—from which to perceive, as through the eye of reason, things-as-they-might-be. The Baconian axiom, "knowledge is power," became the core of his faith; and he was never more typically a man of the Enlightenment than in his conviction that reason and inquiry would lead men away from whatever was false or capricious or twisted in human affairs toward the truth inherent in the natural order of things. With this went a tendency, already evident in law and architecture, to run everything back to its source, whence its inner nature could be defined, and to proceed from that point. A radical tendency, it would usually have radical effects. . . .

A close companion of Jefferson's intellectuality was a characteristic forbearance and reserve in his intercourse with his fellow men. In part, this simply expressed his deference to the forms and proprieties of civilized society; but there was an added quality of austerity in Jefferson that, by Virginia standards, seemed more in keeping with the Puritan type. He was by all appearances an amiable and sociable person, never harsh or disagreeable, and he had a remarkable talent, seemingly effortless in its motions, for drawing men to him. But appearances could be deceiving. . . . He did not lack a sense of humor, yet it could not be considered a strong point of his personality. He was too fussy. What was ludicrous in life was more likely to be cause for regret than amusement. Expecting so much of men, and of nations too, he could not laugh at their follies, least of all at his own. . . . It remains to be seen what effect these traits would have in his public career. But one thing seems clear: he was not, in his nature, born for the public. . . . None of the heroes of his early life was associated with political power. Intellectual and moral power yes, power of state no. Like Seneca, he would "rather be quiet than in arms." And when arms swept him up, he could never resign himself to his fate. He held back, begrudging commitment to the public role, yet unable to make it in any other; and this pattern of forbearance, with its cycles of withdrawal and return, ran through his life.

No less characteristic was Jefferson's penchant for methodical industry, order, and system. In this he proved to be a rigorous man of business, like his father. He hated idleness. He was fond of detail. His personal records—Account Book, Garden Book, Farm Book, and so on—exhibit a profusion of minutiae. He recorded from year to year, for instance, the exact time and place of planting a given vegetable, when it sprouted, when it ripened and came to the table. His meteorological observations, regularly three times a day, extended over several decades. All was neatly ordered and arranged. He enjoyed poetry when young and headstrong, even wrote a verse or two; but he was not a poet by nature and, as he matured, had little call for this muse. In nothing he undertook did he lack facts; and he felt more at home in the realm of empirical data than in the realm of abstractions. The logic of facts took nothing for granted. It dissolved phenomena into component elements, analyzed them, defined their natural relationship, then reconstructed the parts to express the newly discovered truth. Such at least was the intent. Clarity, precision, proportion—these qualities of his architecture expressed an essentially mathematical spirit. . . . Jefferson could not surrender gracefully to life. His whole tendency was to combat the chaos of experience and submit it to the dictates of reason which, of course, he identified with the laws of nature.

Related to this, though seemingly at odds with the traits of intellectuality and reserve, was the fundamentally activist temper of Jefferson's mind. With him, as with enlightened thinkers generally, ideas were meant to act on the world, not simply to reflect it. This functional interest in ideas exalted useful knowledge, practical workmanship, and mastery of nature. Even in the arts he was not primarily a passive observer or auditor; his greatest enjoyment came from participation. His temperament rejected the conventional dualism of mind and body, thought and work, theory and practice. He espoused bodily health and activity as the necessary condition of mental vigor; and partly for the same reason, he distrusted overly civilized environments cut off from physical nature. He loved to tinker, to work with his hands, as Monticello would demonstrate. The versatility that would become one of his claims to fame, the result of the workman-like temperament nurtured by his own environment, was already evident in the young Jefferson who, in James Parton's memorable description, "could calculate an eclipse, survey an estate, tie an artery, plan an edifice, try a cause, break a horse, dance a minuet, and play a violin."

An activist must, of necessity, be an optimist as well. The world of experience was malleable to the hammers of the mind. Only gloomy and hypochondriac souls thought differently. "My temperament is sanguine," Jefferson told John Adams in his seventy-third year, and he might have said the same thing in his thirtieth. "I steer my bark with Hope in the head, leaving Fear astern."

The most fortunate of us, in our journey through life, frequently meet with calamities and misfortunes which may greatly afflict us; and, to fortify our minds against the attacks of these calamities and misfortunes, should be one of the principal studies and endeavors of our lives. The only method of doing this is to assume a perfect resignation to the Divine will, to consider that whatever does happen, must happen; and that, by our uneasiness, we cannot prevent the blow before it does fall, but we may add to its force after it has fallen. These considerations, and others such as these, may enable us in some measure to surmount the difficulties thrown in our way; to bear up with a tolerable degree of patience under this burthen of life; and to proceed with a pious and unshaken resignation, till we arrive at our journey's end, when we may deliver up our trust into the hands of him who gave it, and receive such reward as to him shall seem proportioned to our merit. Such, dear Page, will be the language of the man who considers his situation in this life, and such should be the language of every man who would wish to render that situation as easy as the nature of it will admit. Few things will disturb him at all: nothing will disturb him much.

Thomas Jefferson, from a letter to John Page, July 15, 1763

JEFFERSON THE PATRIOT
1769-1781

Thomas Jefferson began his political career in 1769, when he became a member of the Virginia House of Burgesses. Merely intending to fulfill the civic duty incumbent upon an educated landowner, Jefferson stepped onto the public stage at a dramatic turning point in colonial history—the moment when longstanding unrest was about to foment a revolution. For Jefferson, who believed passionately in the natural rights of the individual and the perfectibility of human society, the colonial cause was a real life test of his most dearly held beliefs. In the years between 1769 and 1781, Jefferson emerged as the voice of the American Revolution, the man whose words gave eloquent voice to the struggle for independence.

At left, a stipple engraving of Thomas Jefferson by David Edwin (after Rembrandt Peale). National Portrait Gallery, Smithsonian Institution/Art Resource, NY. At right, a 1778 view of Philadelphia by an unknown artist. Photo Michael Sheldon, Art Resource, NY.

A Member of the Legislature

Thomas Jefferson, from his *Autobiography*

1769
TJ becomes a member of the Virginia House of Burgesses.

1769
Daniel Boone enters Kentucky Territory.

1770
Fire destroys Shadwell, the Jefferson family home.

1770
In what becomes known as the Boston Massacre, British soldiers kill five colonists and injure six.

1770
The Townshend Acts are repealed by the British Parliament, eliminating duties on imports to the colonies; only the tax on tea is maintained.

1771
Benjamin Franklin begins his autobiography.

1772
TJ marries Martha Wayles Skelton at her father's Virginia home, The Forest.

1772
TJ helps form the Virginia Committee of Correspondence to facilitate communication with other colonies.

1772
The British ship Gaspee is burned by American colonists in Providence, Rhode Island.

1773
British Parliament passes the Tea Act to promote British tea and to destroy colonial competition for the tea market.

1773
Colonists dressed as Indians board British ships in Boston Harbor and throw 342 casks of tea overboard.

Jefferson became a member of the Virginia House of Burgesses in 1769. The body's power was limited, subject to the veto of the royal governor and review by the King's Privy Council. In 1772, Jefferson helped found the Committees of Correspondence to facilitate communication between the colonies, and in 1774 he led Virginia's bold response to the Boston Port Act, a British law aimed at punishing Massachusetts for its revolt over tea taxes. This excerpt from Jefferson's Autobiography *traces the emergence of his political career as the colonies moved toward unity in opposition to the Crown and began to make plans for the First Continental Congress.*

In 1769 I became a member of the legislature by the choice of the county in which I live, and so continued until it was closed by the Revolution. . . . Our minds were circumscribed within narrow limits by a habitual belief that it was our duty to be subordinate to the mother country in all matters of government, to direct all our labors in subservience to her interests, and even to observe a bigoted intolerance for all religions but hers. The difficulties with our representatives were of habit and despair, not of reflection and conviction. Experience soon proved that they could bring their minds to rights on the first summons of their attention. But the King's Council, which acted as another house of legislature, held their places at will, and were in most humble obedience to that will; the Governor too, who had a negative on our laws, held by the same tenure, and with still greater devotedness to it; and, last of all, the Royal negative closed the last door to every hope of amelioration. . . .

In May, 1769, a meeting of the General Assembly was called . . . and to that meeting became known the joint resolutions and address of the Lords and Commons of 1768–9, on the proceedings in Massachusetts. Counter-resolutions and an address to the King by the House of Burgesses were agreed to with little opposition, and a spirit manifestly displayed itself of considering the cause of Massachusetts as a common one. The Governor dissolved us, but we met the next day in the Apollo of the Raleigh Tavern, formed ourselves into a voluntary convention, drew up articles of association against the use of any merchandise imported from Great Britain, signed and recommended them to the people. . . .

Nothing of particular excitement occurring for a considerable time, our countrymen seemed to fall into a state of insensibility to our situation; the duty on tea, not yet repealed, and the Declaratory Act of a right in the British Parliament to bind us by their laws in all cases whatsoever still suspended over us. . . . Not thinking our old and leading members up to the point of forwardness and zeal which the times required, Mr. Henry, Richard Henry Lee, Francis L. Lee, Mr. Carr and myself agreed to meet in the evening, in a private room of the Raleigh, to consult on the state of things. . . . We were all sensible that the most urgent of all measures was that of coming to an understanding with all the other colonies to consider the British claims as a common cause to all, and to produce a unity of action; and, for this purpose, that a committee of correspondence in each colony would be the best instrument for intercommunication and that their first measure would probably be to propose a meeting of deputies from every colony, at some central place, who should be charged with the direction of the measures which should be taken by all. We, therefore, drew up . . . resolutions . . . and a committee of correspondence [was] appointed of whom Peyton Randolph, the speaker, was chairman. The Governor . . . dissolved us, but the committee met the next day, prepared a circular letter to the speakers of the other colonies, inclosing to each a copy of the resolutions, and left it in charge with their chairman to forward them by expresses. . . .

The next event which excited our sympathies for Massachusetts was the Boston Port Bill, by which that port was to be shut up on the 1st of June, 1774. This arrived while we were in session in the spring of that year. The lead in the House on these subjects being no longer left to the old members, Mr. Henry, R. H. Lee, Fr. L. Lee, three or four other members whom I do not recollect, and myself, agreeing that we must boldly take an unequivocal stand in the line with Massachusetts, determined to meet and consult on the proper measures in the council-chamber. . . . We were under conviction of the necessity of arousing our people from the lethargy into which they had fallen as to passing events, and thought that the appointment of a day of general fasting and prayer would be most likely to call up and alarm their attention.

. . . We cooked up a resolution . . . for appointing the 1st day of June, on which the Port Bill was to commence, for a day of fasting, humiliation, and prayer to implore Heaven to avert from us the evils of civil war, to inspire us with firmness in support of our rights, and to turn the hearts of the King and Parliament to moderation and justice. To give greater emphasis to our proposition, we agreed to wait the next morning on Mr. Nicholas, whose grave and religious character was more in unison with the tone of our resolution, and to solicit him to move it. We accordingly went to him in the morning. He moved it the same day; the 1st of June was proposed; and it passed without opposition. The Governor dissolved us, as usual.

We retired to the Apollo, as before, agreed to an association, and instructed the committee of correspondence to propose to the corresponding committees of the other colonies to appoint deputies to meet in Congress at such place, *annually,* as should be convenient, to direct from time to time the measures required by the general interest; and we declared that an attack on any one colony should be considered as an attack on the whole. . . . We further recommended to the several counties to elect deputies to meet at Williamsburg the 1st of August ensuing, to consider the state of the colony, and particularly to appoint delegates to a general Congress, should that measure be acceded to by the committees of correspondence generally. It was acceded to; Philadelphia was appointed for the place, and the 5th of September for the time of the meeting. We returned home and in our several counties invited the clergy to meet assemblies of the people on the 1st of June to perform the ceremonies of the day, and to address to them discourses suited to the occasion. The people met generally, with anxiety and alarm in their countenances, and the effect of the day through the whole colony was like a shock of electricity, arousing every man and placing him erect and solidly on his centre. They chose, universally, delegates for the convention. Being elected one for my own county, I prepared a draught of instructions to be given to the delegates whom we should send to the Congress, which I meant to propose at our meeting.

The question, who commenced the Revolution? is as difficult as that of the first inventors of a thousand good things. For example, who first discovered the principle of gravity? Not Newton; for Galileo, who died the year Newton was born, had measured its force in the descent of gravid bodies. . . . The fact is that one new idea leads to another, that to a third, and so on through a course of time until someone, with whom no one of these ideas was original, combines all together and produces what is justly called a new invention. I suppose it would be as difficult to trace our Revolution to its first embryo. . . . The truth, I suppose, is that the opposition in every colony began whenever the encroachment was presented to it. This question of priority is as the inquiry would be who first, of the three hundred Spartans, offered his name to Leonidas?

Thomas Jefferson, from a letter to Dr. Benjamin Waterhouse, March 3, 1818

During his days as a student at William and Mary, Jefferson attended dances at Williamsburg's Raleigh Tavern. As a member of the House of Burgesses, however, he took up far more serious business inside the Raleigh. After the Virginia House of Burgesses was formally dissolved by King George, Jefferson and a group of fellow legislators met inside the Raleigh's Apollo Room to discuss plans for unifying the colonies in opposition to British transgressions of their rights. Above, the sign outside Williamsburg's Raleigh Tavern. Photo SuperStock.

FROM *A SUMMARY VIEW OF THE RIGHTS OF BRITISH AMERICA*

BY THOMAS JEFFERSON

Our ancestors, before their emigration to America, were the free inhabitants of the British dominions in Europe, and possessed a right, which nature has given to all men, of departing from the country in which chance, not choice, has placed them, of going in quest of new habitations, and of there establishing new societies, under such laws and regulations as, to them, shall seem most likely to promote public happiness. . . . Settlement having been thus effected in the wilds of America, the emigrants thought proper to adopt that system of laws, under which they had hitherto lived in the mother country, and to continue their union with her, by submitting themselves to the same common sovereign, who was thereby made the central link, connecting the several parts of the empire thus newly multiplied.

Thomas Jefferson, from A Summary View of the Rights of British America

The Virginia House of Burgesses met in Williamsburg in August 1774, to choose delegates for the Continental Congress. Jefferson was not present, nor was he chosen as a delegate; but he did send to Williamsburg two copies of a document that explained his current feelings about the king, the colonies, and the rights of man. That paper, given the title A Summary View of the Rights of British America, *was not formally considered by the burgesses—it was passed over as too radical; but Jefferson's ideas did find an audience, and would soon be embraced throughout the colonies. Below, in closing his paper, Jefferson insists that separation is not the colonies' desire, but neither will they surrender their rights in the name of preserving the peace.*

These are our grievances, which we have thus laid before his Majesty, with that freedom of language and sentiment which becomes a free people claiming their rights as derived from the laws of nature, and not as the gift of their Chief Magistrate. Let those flatter, who fear: it is not an American art. To give praise where it is not due might be well from the venal, but would ill beseem those who are asserting the rights of human nature. They know, and will, therefore, say, that Kings are the servants, not the proprietors of the people. Open your breast, Sire, to liberal and expanded thought. . . . The whole art of government consists in the art of being honest. Only aim to do your duty, and mankind will give you credit where you fail. No longer persevere in sacrificing the rights of one part of the empire to the inordinate desires of another; but deal out to all, equal and impartial right. Let no act be passed by any one legislature, which may infringe on the rights and liberties of another. This is the important post in which fortune has placed you, holding the balance of a great, if a well-poised empire. This, Sire, is the advice of your great American council, on the observance of which may perhaps depend your felicity and future fame, and the preservation of that harmony which alone can continue, both to Great Britain and America, the reciprocal advantages of their connection. It is neither our wish nor our interest to separate from her. We are willing, on our part, to sacrifice everything which reason can ask, to the restoration of that tranquillity for which all must wish. On their part, let them be ready to establish union on a generous plan. Let them name their terms, but let them be just. Accept of every commercial preference it is in our power to give, for such things as we can raise for their use, or they make for ours. But let them not think to exclude us from going to other markets to dispose of those commodities which they cannot use, nor to supply those wants which they cannot supply. Still less, let it be proposed, that our properties, within our own territories, shall be taxed or regulated by any power on earth but our own. The God who gave us life, gave us liberty at the same time: the hand of force may destroy, but cannot disjoin them. This, Sire, is our last, our determined resolution. And that you will be pleased to interpose, with that efficacy which your earnest endeavors may insure, to procure redress of these our great grievances, to quiet the minds of your subjects in British America against any apprehensions of future encroachment, to establish fraternal love and harmony through the whole empire, and that that may continue to the latest ages of time, is the fervent prayer of all British America.

JEFFERSON IN THE CONTINENTAL CONGRESS
FROM *IN PURSUIT OF REASON,* BY NOBLE E. CUNNINGHAM

In September of 1774, while Jefferson remained in Virginia, the First Continental Congress met in Philadelphia. The delegates reaffirmed their unified opposition to the continued violations of their rights by the British Crown, and they also signed a non-importation, non-consumption, non-exportation agreement which was meant to prove their seriousness and solidarity. The delegates agreed to meet again the following spring; it was at that spring meeting, as a late replacement for a delegate called away on Virginia business, that Jefferson became a member of the Continental Congress. Fighting had already begun in Massachusetts. Jefferson stepped into the midst of a revolution.

It was June 21, 1775, when Jefferson arrived in Philadelphia after a ten-day journey from Williamsburg. While he was en route, the Continental Congress named George Washington the commander in chief of all continental forces. Two days after Jefferson's arrival the general departed for Boston amid bands playing and an outpouring of public support. "The war is now heartily entered into," Jefferson wrote, "without a prospect of accommodation but thro' the effectual interposition of arms."

The second Continental Congress had been sitting since May 10, and John Hancock

On December 16, 1773, a group of Massachusetts patriots dressed as Indians boarded a British ship docked in Boston Harbor and threw its cargo of tea overboard. Their actions were in response to the British Parliament's manipulation of tea taxes to favor English exporters. The Boston Tea Party, as it soon became known, brought down the wrath of the Crown upon Massachusetts, but it also rallied colonists up and down the Eastern Seaboard in defense of colonial rights. Among the most fervent supporters of the Boston patriots was Jefferson, who led a movement in the Virginia House of Burgesses for an official show of support by Virginians for Massachusetts. Above, an unknown artist's depiction of the Boston Tea Party. Photo A.K.G., Berlin/SuperStock.

A Summary View of the Rights of British America was indeed a bold statement. Although too extreme for 1774, it would not long be so regarded. Its circulation propelled Jefferson into the front ranks of the champions of American rights and established those credentials that two years later placed him on the committee to draft the Declaration of Independence. In addition to a broad statement of principles, Jefferson presented a detailed enumeration of American grievances against both Parliament and the crown, formulating the list of charges that he would add to and incorporate into the Declaration of Independence. Jefferson based A Summary View on the contention that the only connection between the settlements in America and Great Britain was through the crown. . . .

Most Americans in 1774 were not ready to go so far as the thirty-one-year-old Albemarle delegate. That was evident in the resolutions adopted by the Virginia convention, which were primarily concerned with creating a vigorous nonimportation association and halting all exports of tobacco and other products to Great Britain after August 10, 1775, if American grievances were not redressed by then. Some Virginians in fact used Jefferson's paper to emphasize the moderation of the convention's approach. In a preface added upon publication, the editors applauded the "faithful accuracy" with which the sources of the differences with Great Britain were examined and the "manly firmness" with which "the opinions entertained by every free American" were expressed. Then they added, "It will evince to the world the moderation of our late convention, who have only touched with tenderness many of the claims insisted on in this pamphlet, though every heart acknowledged their justice."

Noble E. Cunningham, from In Pursuit of Reason

The next gale that sweeps from the North will bring to our ears the clash of resounding arms! Our brethren are already in the field! Why stand we here idle? What is it that gentlemen wish? What would they have? Is life so dear, or peace so sweet, as to be purchased at the price of chains and slavery? Forbid it, Almighty God! I know not what course others may take; but as for me, give me liberty, or give me death!

Patrick Henry, from a speech to the Second Virginia Convention, March 23, 1775

In May of 1765, when Jefferson was a law student in Williamsburg, he stood in the gallery during a meeting of the House of Burgesses and heard a young delegate named Patrick Henry vigorously object to the Stamp Act. Jefferson, impressed by Henry's eloquence, later recalled that he spoke "as Homer wrote." In years to come, Jefferson would join Henry as one of the more radical members of the House of Burgesses, but the two men would never become close friends. Henry was a country lawyer with a flair for the dramatic. He had risen from poverty and remained throughout his life rather rough around the edges. Jefferson, by contrast, was naturally reserved and refined and preferred to speak his mind through the written word. The day would come when the two would find themselves at odds; nonetheless, Jefferson's first impression never changed. Late in his life, Jefferson told Henry's biographer that Henry was the greatest orator who ever lived. Portrait by James Barton Longacre, National Portrait Gallery, Smithsonian Institution/Art Resource, NY.

was now presiding, having succeeded to the chair when Peyton Randolph returned to Williamsburg. Jefferson was well acquainted with the Virginia delegation, which after Washington's departure included Richard Henry Lee, Patrick Henry, Richard Bland, Benjamin Harrison, and Edmund Pendleton. But among some fifty other delegates there was no one whom he had ever seen before. The reputations of the leading men, though, were known to him, and he must have been as anxious to meet Samuel Adams, Benjamin Franklin, John Adams, and others as they were curious to see the young Virginian whose reputation as a spokesman for colonial rights had preceded him. Jefferson had become known especially through his *Summary View of the Rights of British America*, which had circulated during the previous Congress. Samuel Ward, a delegate from Rhode Island, wrote just after Jefferson's first appearance in Congress: "Yesterday the famous Mr. Jefferson a Delegate from Virginia in the Room of Mr. Randolph arrived. . . . He looks like a very sensible spirited fine Fellow and by the Pamphlet which he wrote last Summer he certainly is one." Jefferson brought to Congress, John Adams said, "a reputation for literature, science, and a happy talent of composition. Writings of his were handed about, remarkable for the peculiar felicity of expression." Adams also said that Jefferson never spoke in the debates and "during the whole Time I satt [*sic*] with him in Congress, I never heard him utter three Sentences together." At the same time, Adams recalled that Jefferson "was so prompt, frank, explicit and decisive upon committees and in conversation . . . that he soon seized upon my heart."

Jefferson's talents as a writer were called upon shortly after he took his seat in Congress. On June 23, two days following his arrival, Congress named a committee to draw up a declaration to be published by General Washington upon taking command of the forces before Boston. When the committee's draft was presented to Congress, it was recommitted and Jefferson and John Dickinson were added to the committee. Jefferson then wrote a new draft drawing heavily on his *Summary View*, though with a far less declamatory tone than employed earlier. The committee was not yet satisfied and gave Jefferson's draft to Dickinson to rework before submitting the declaration to Congress on July 6. Congress spent the day debating it paragraph by paragraph and approved the manifesto with only slight modification. . . . John Adams said of the declaration: "It has Some Mercury in it, and is pretty frank, plain, and clear. If Lord North dont [*sic*] compliment every Mother's Son of us, with a Bill of Attainder, in Exchange for it, I shall think it owing to Fear."

Accounts of the fighting at Bunker Hill had reached Philadelphia by the time Jefferson wrote to Albemarle neighbor George Gilmer on July 5. He praised the valor of New Englanders and reported heavy losses sustained by the British. While not at liberty to reveal all of the proceedings of the Congress, he could let it be known that Congress had directed the raising of twenty thousand troops and that most of them had already been enlisted. The news was encouraging to Gilmer, who was encamped with a company of Albemarle volunteers outside Williamsburg when Jefferson's letter reached him, but he was alarmed by Jefferson's report of a shortage of gunpowder. On the whole, though, Jefferson's letter was an optimistic one that reported that "nobody now entertains a doubt but that we are able to cope with the whole force of Great Britain, if we are but willing to exert ourselves." The war would be expensive, he said, but individuals would have to sacrifice their private interests. "As our enemies have found we can reason like men," he declared, "so now let us show them we can fight like men also." Gilmer was not the only person to read these stirring words, for the main text of Jefferson's letter was published in Williamsburg on July 28 in Purdie's *Virginia Gazette* as an "extract of a letter from one of the Virginia delegates."

At the same time that they approved the forceful "Declaration of the Causes and Necessity of taking up Arms," members of Congress endorsed a second petition to King George III, and forty-nine delegates, including Jefferson, signed it on July 8. Jefferson recalled that John Dickinson, who had drafted it, signed with much satisfaction, but that some members—among whom he included himself—did so with less enthusiasm. The Virginia delegation certainly put little faith in its success when they reported it to the Virginia convention, for they followed it with an urgent plea for military preparations.

More significant than the petition to the king was Congress' response to Lord North's conciliatory proposal, which had been referred to the continental body by the assemblies of New Jersey, Pennsylvania, and Virginia. On July 22 Benjamin Franklin, Jefferson, John Adams, and Richard Henry Lee were appointed a committee to report on North's proposition. Because Jefferson had drafted the Virginia response and had brought a copy with him, he was delegated the task of drafting the committee's report. Other committee members contributed suggestions, and Congress made some changes before final adoption, but the main lines of the resolutions approved by Congress on July 31 followed Jefferson's draft. He in turn drew on the paper he had prepared for the Virginia House of Burgesses. The result was a vigorous rejection of North's proposal as unreasonable, insidious, and altogether unsatisfactory.

During his first six weeks in Congress, Jefferson thus had a leading role in drafting two major state papers adopted by Congress. Both the "Declaration of the Causes and Necessity of taking up Arms" and the response to Lord North's conciliatory plan would be widely published in newspapers throughout the colonies. Jefferson's name was not publicly associated with either of these declarations, which came from Congress, but to members of that body the papers were early demonstrations of Jefferson's literary and polemical abilities and of his commitment to the American cause. Six weeks after leaving Virginia, he was among the leading men in Congress and in the front ranks of the revolutionists.

The proposition seems also to have been calculated more particularly to lull into fatal security our well-affected fellow subjects on the other side of the water till time should be given for the operation of those arms which a British minister pronounced would instantaneously reduce the "cowardly" sons of America to unreserved submission. But when the world reflects how inadequate to justice are these vaunted terms; when it attends to the rapid and bold succession of injuries which during the course of eleven years have been aimed at these colonies; when it reviews the pacific and respectful expostulations which during that whole time were the sole arms we opposed to them; when it observes that our complaints were either not heard at all or were answered with new and accumulated injuries; when it recollects that the minister himself on an early occasion declared "that he would never treat with America, till he had brought her to her feet," and that an avowed partisan of ministry has more lately denounced against us the dreadful sentence, "Let Carthage be destroyed"; . . . when it considers the great armaments with which they have invaded us and the circumstances of cruelty with which these have commenced and prosecuted hostilities; when these things, we say, are laid together and attentively considered, can the world be deceived into an opinion that we are unreasonable, or can it hesitate to believe with us that nothing but our own exertions may defeat the ministerial sentence of death or abject submission?

from the reply to Lord North, drafted by a committee including Jefferson in response to an offer of reconciliation made by the British prime minister in May of 1775

The First Continental Congress met in Philadelphia's Carpenter's Hall in 1774. In 1775, the body met at the State House, which would soon earn the name Independence Hall, in honor of the debate over and signing of the Declaration of Independence which took place within its walls. Even after the Revolution, Philadelphia remained the center of American government. The Constitutional Convention was held in the city, and Philadelphia was the seat of the nation's government during the 1790s, before the new capital city of Washington, D.C., was completed. At left, artist Ferdinand Reichardt's depiction of Philadelphia, including Independence Hall, in 1858. Photo SuperStock.

FROM THE CAUSES AND NECESSITIES OF TAKING UP ARMS
THOMAS JEFFERSON AND JOHN DICKINSON

1774

Britain closes the port of Boston in June to punish the colony for the Boston Tea Party; TJ helps organize a day of fasting and prayer in Virginia to demonstrate solidarity with Massachusetts.

1774

TJ writes A Summary View of the Rights of British America at Monticello.

1774

The First Continental Congress convenes in Philadelphia, Pennsylvania.

1775

The first abolitionist society is organized in America.

1775

TJ is among the audience as Patrick Henry delivers his "Give me liberty, or give me death" speech at the Second Virginia Convention in Richmond.

1775

Daniel Boone begins blazing the Wilderness Road from Virginia into Kentucky; thereafter, it becomes the main route for westward traffic.

1775

The American Revolution begins in Lexington and Concord, Massachusetts.

I hold it, that a little rebellion, now and then, is a good thing, and as necessary in the political world as storms in the physical. Unsuccessful rebellions, indeed, generally establish the encroachments on the rights of the people, which have produced them. An observation of this truth should render honest republican governors so mild in their punishment of rebellions, as not to discourage them too much. It is a medicine necessary for the sound health of government.

Thomas Jefferson, from a letter to James Madison, January 30, 1787

The Declaration of the Causes and Necessities of Taking up Arms, approved by the Continental Congress on July 6, 1775, held out hope of reconciliation with Great Britain, but stated that continued transgressions of colonial rights had made armed opposition the proper response.

We are reduced to the alternative of choosing an unconditional submission to the tyranny of irritated ministers, or resistance by force. The latter is our choice. We have counted the cost of this contest, and find nothing so dreadful as voluntary slavery. Honor, justice, and humanity forbid us tamely to surrender that freedom which we received from our gallant ancestors, and which our innocent posterity have a right to receive from us. . . .

Our cause is just. Our union is perfect. Our internal resources are great, and, if necessary, foreign assistance is undoubtedly attainable. We gratefully acknowledge, as signal instances of the Divine favor towards us, that His Providence would not permit us to be called into this severe controversy until we were grown up to our present strength, had been previously exercised in warlike operation, and possessed of the means of defending ourselves. With hearts fortified with these animating reflections, we most solemnly, before God and the world, declare that, exerting the utmost energy of those powers which our beneficent Creator hath graciously bestowed upon us, the arms we have been compelled by our enemies to assume we will, in defiance of every hazard, with unabating firmness and perseverance, employ for the preservation of our liberties; being with one mind resolved to die freemen rather than to live slaves.

Lest this declaration should disquiet the minds of our friends and fellow-subjects in any part of the empire, we assure them that we mean not to dissolve that union which has so long and so happily subsisted between us and which we sincerely wish to see restored. Necessity has not yet driven us into that desperate measure, or induced us to excite any other nation to war against them. We have not raised armies with ambitious designs of separating from Great Britain and establishing independent states. We fight not for glory or for conquest. We exhibit to mankind the remarkable spectacle of a people attacked by unprovoked enemies, without any imputation or even suspicion of offense. They boast of their privileges and civilization, and yet proffer no milder conditions than servitude or death.

In our native land, in defense of the freedom that is our birthright and which we ever enjoyed till the late violation of it; for the protection of our property, acquired solely by the honest industry of our forefathers and ourselves; against violence actually offered; we have taken up arms. We shall lay them down when hostilities shall cease on the part of the aggressors and all danger of their being renewed shall be removed, and not before.

With a humble confidence in the mercies of the supreme and impartial Judge and Ruler of the Universe, we most devoutly implore His divine goodness to protect us happily through this great conflict, to dispose our adversaries to reconciliation on reasonable terms, and thereby to relieve the empire from the calamities of civil war.

John Dickinson, above, was a Philadelphia lawyer who earned the nickname "Penman of the Revolution" for the many documents he wrote during the years leading up to the Revolution. Along with the Declaration of the Causes and Necessities of Taking Up Arms, which he co-wrote with Jefferson, Dickinson wrote Letters from a Farmer in Pennsylvania and a popular song called "The Liberty Song," both of which served to stir up colonists against the injustices of the British Crown. But Dickinson was not a fervent supporter of independence. He remained hopeful of reconciliation to the end and gave up his seat in the Pennsylvania delegation at the Continental Congress when it became certain that the Declaration of Independence would be approved. In his last speech to that body, delivered just before July 4, 1776, Dickinson warned of the grave dangers of separating from Great Britain. His words had little effect on Jefferson and others who had long since committed to full independence. Stipple engraving of John Dickinson by Burnet Reading (after du Simitiere), National Portrait Gallery, Smithsonian Insititution, Washington, D.C. Photo Art Resource.

"O ye that love mankind! Ye that dare oppose not only the tyranny but the tyrant, stand forth! Every spot of the old world is overrun with oppression. Freedom hath been hunted round the globe. Asia and Africa have long expelled her. Europe regards her like a stranger, and England hath given her warning to depart. O receive the fugitive, and prepare in time an asylum for mankind." So wrote Thomas Paine in January 1776, in his best-selling pamphlet, Common Sense, which was the first open call in the colonies for independence from Great Britain. Paine continued to rouse the colonists later in 1776 with the publication of The Crisis. Years later, after he was convicted of treason in Great Britain for a pamphlet called The Rights of Man, Paine lived in France and corresponded with Jefferson. He returned to the United States in 1802, where he lived until his death in 1809. Above, George Romney's engraving of Paine. Bibliotheque Nationale, Paris. Giraudon/Art Resource, NY.

AUTHOR OF INDEPENDENCE

FROM *IN PURSUIT OF REASON*, BY NOBLE E. CUNNINGHAM

1775

The Second Continental Congress meets in Philadelphia in May.

1775

TJ arrives in Philadelphia as a delegate to the Second Continental Congress in June.

1775

TJ helps draft the reply to Lord North's proposal for reconciliation.

1775

TJ and John Dickinson write the Declaration of the Causes and Necessities of Taking up Arms.

1775

George Washington is named commander-in-chief of the Continental Army.

Believe me, dear Sir, there is not in the British empire a man who more cordially loves a union with Great Britain than I do. But by the God that made me, I will cease to exist before I yield to a connection on such terms as the British Parliament propose; and in this, I think I speak the sentiments of America. We want neither inducement nor power, to declare and assert a separation. It is will, alone, which is wanting, and that is growing apace under the fostering hand of our King. One bloody campaign will probably decide, everlastingly, our future course; and I am sorry to find a bloody campaign is decided on. If our winds and waters should not combine to rescue their shores from slavery, and General Howe's reinforcements should arrive in safety, we have hopes he will be inspirited to come out of Boston and take another drubbing; and we must drub him soundly before the sceptred tyrant will know we are not mere brutes, to crouch under his hand, and kiss the rod with which he designs to scourge us.

Thomas Jefferson, from a letter to John Randolph

After an interlude at his work-in-progress home at Monticello, Jefferson returned to the Continental Congress in May of 1776. The mood was ripe for action. Thomas Paine's pamphlet, Common Sense, *had been published in January, rousing the colonists and rallying public opinion behind the cause of independence from Great Britain. The time had come for a bold, decisive move. A special committee of the Continental Congress chose Thomas Jefferson to prepare the first draft of a document announcing and justifying the colonies' claim of independence.*

On June 7, 1776, Richard Henry Lee introduced in Congress the resolution "That these United Colonies are, and of right ought to be, free and independent States, that they are absolved from all allegiance to the British Crown, and that all political connection between them and the State of Great Britain is, and ought to be, totally dissolved." Congress considered this resolution on June 8 and again on June 10, when action on it was postponed until July 1. In the course of these debates it appeared that some colonies "were not yet matured for falling from the parent stem," Jefferson noted, "but that they were fast advancing to that state," and "it was thought most prudent to wait a while for them." It was not a question of whether the resolution would pass or fail, for its adoption was not in doubt. What was sought was unanimity.

Meanwhile, a committee was appointed on June 11 to draft a declaration to announce and justify the anticipated act. The committee, composed of Thomas Jefferson, John Adams, Benjamin Franklin, Roger Sherman, and Robert R. Livingston, delegated to Jefferson the task of preparing a draft. He did so, working alone in his lodgings, using a portable lap desk recently made to his specifications by a Philadelphia cabinetmaker. Why was Jefferson chosen to do the drafting? In old age Adams said that he and Jefferson had been named a subcommittee to prepare a draft and each had pressed the other to do so. . . .

When Jefferson learned of Adams's recollections, he said Adams was mistaken. There had never been any subcommittee, and it was the entire committee that "unanimously pressed on myself alone to undertake the draught." Jefferson said that at age eighty he would not claim any advantage of memory over Adams at eighty-eight, but he insisted that his notes made at the time did not support Adams's version. Though Adams may have recorded an imaginary conversation, the reasons that he gave for Jefferson being chosen to draft the Declaration ring true. He probably remembered a subcommittee because, after preparing his draft, Jefferson submitted it separately to Adams and to Franklin for their suggestions and corrections before presenting it to the full committee. Both men made alterations in their own handwriting on Jefferson's draft, producing a unique and historic document that still survives today. Jefferson then made a fair copy for the committee, which made a few changes and reported it to Congress on June 28.

Before considering Jefferson's Declaration, Congress had to act on Lee's resolution for independence and resumed debate on it on July 1. The following day it was adopted with the affirmative votes of all delegations except New York, whose delegates were bound by instructions that obligated them to abstain. By July 15 they would receive new instructions and make approval of independence unanimous. Debate on the Declaration of Independence began on July 2 and continued through three days. In the course of the debates, Congress considerably altered Jefferson's draft as approved by the committee, cutting about a quarter of the text, polishing the wording, and in some instances making substantive changes. The most significant alteration came when Congress struck from Jefferson's text his condemnation of George III for allowing the slave trade to continue—a strongly worded passage in which Jefferson had denounced the slave trade as a "cruel war against human nature itself." Jefferson said the change was made in compliance with the wishes of South Carolina and Georgia but added that "our Northern brethren also I believe felt a little tender under those censures; for tho' their people have very few slaves themselves yet they had been pretty considerable carriers of them to others." Most of the changes that Congress made in shortening and revising the wording of the document improved it, though the sensitive author believed that his draft was the stronger statement. When he sent copies of the Declaration as approved by Congress to a few of his friends, he sent a paper showing the original draft and the alterations so they could judge whether it was made better or worse by his critics. After the various revisions were made, Congress adopted the Declaration on July 4. . . .

Despite the changes made by the committee and by Congress in his draft, Jefferson could still rightly claim authorship of the Declaration of Independence, and he would subsequently come to regard it as one of the three most important accomplishments of his life. The sources of the ideas that Jefferson drew on in writing the Declaration would later become a source of interest to his contemporaries and of continuing fascination to historians. Richard Henry Lee thought Jefferson had copied from John Locke's treatise on government. John Adams in old age charged that the essence of Jefferson's ideas could be found in fellow New Englander James Otis's pamphlet *The Rights of the British Colonies Asserted and Proved* (Boston, 1764). When Jefferson heard this, he said flatly that he had never seen Otis's pamphlet. He did not deny that he had read Locke, but he insisted that he had "turned to neither book nor pamphlet while writing it." At the same time, Jefferson claimed no originality for the Declaration of Independence. "I did not consider it as any part of my charge to invent new ideas altogether, and to offer no sentiment which had ever been expressed before," he said. His aim was "to place before mankind the common sense of the subject, in terms so plain and firm as to command their assent," and to justify independence. "Neither aiming at originality of principle or sentiment, nor yet copied from any particular and previous writing," he wrote, "it was intended to be an expression of the American mind."

You inquire why so young a man as Mr. Jefferson was placed at the head of the Committee for preparing a Declaration of Independence? . . . Mr. Jefferson came into Congress, in June, 1775, and brought with him a reputation for literature, science, and a happy talent for composition. Writings of his were handed about, remarkable for the peculiar felicity of expression. Though a silent member of Congress, he was so prompt, frank, explicit, and decisive upon committees and in conversation, not even Samuel Adams was more so, that he soon seized upon my heart; and upon this occasion I gave him my vote, and did all in my power to procure the votes of others. I think he had one more vote than any other, and that placed him at the head of the committee. I had the next highest number, and that placed me the second. The committee met, discussed the subject, and then appointed Mr. Jefferson and me to make the draught, I suppose because we were the two first on the list.

The sub-committee met. Jefferson proposed to me to make the draught. I said, "I will not."

"You should do it," he said.

"Oh! no."

"Why will you not? You ought to do it."

"I will not."

"Why?"

"Reasons enough," I said.

"What can be your reasons?"

"Reason first—You are a Virginian, and a Virginian ought to appear at the head of this business. Reason second—I am obnoxious, suspected, and unpopular. You are very much otherwise. Reason third—You can write ten times better than I can."

"Well," said Jefferson, "if you are decided, I will do as well as I can."

"Very well. When you have drawn it up, we will have a meeting."

John Adams, recollecting the selection of Jefferson to write the first draft of the Declaration of Independence

FROM THE DECLARATION OF INDEPENDENCE

THOMAS JEFFERSON

1776

Common Sense by Thomas Paine is published; the pamphlet contains the first public demand for independence from Great Britain.

1776

British troops evacuate the city of Boston on March 17.

1776

TJ returns to the Continental Congress in May after spending time at Monticello.

1776

On June 7, the Continental Congress hears a resolution that the colonies should declare themselves independent from Great Britain.

1776

TJ prepares the first draft of the Declaration of Independence in Philadelphia during the last weeks of June.

1776

The Continental Congress debates and alters TJ's draft of the Declaration of Independence.

Jefferson's first draft of the Declaration of Independence was altered by the Congress during three days of fierce debate. Perhaps the most significant change was the removal of Jefferson's harsh condemnation of King George for prohibiting the colonies from interfering with the transatlantic slave trade. The revised document was formally adopted on July 4, 1776.

When in the course of human events it becomes necessary for one people to dissolve the political bands which have connected them with another, and to assume among the powers of the earth the separate and equal station to which the laws of nature and of nature's God entitle them, a decent respect to the opinions of mankind requires that they should declare the causes which impel them to the separation.

We hold these truths to be self-evident: that all men are created equal; that they are endowed by their Creator with *certain* inalienable rights; that among these are life, liberty, and the pursuit of happiness; that to secure these rights, governments are instituted among men, deriving their just powers from the consent of the governed; that whenever any form of government becomes destructive of these ends, it is the right of the people to alter or to abolish it, and to institute new government, laying its foundation on such principles, and organizing its powers in such form, as to them shall seem most likely to effect their safety and happiness. Prudence, indeed, will dictate that governments long established should not be changed for light and transient causes; and accordingly all experience hath shown that mankind are more disposed to suffer while evils are sufferable, than to right themselves by abolishing the forms to which they are accustomed. But when a long train of abuses and usurpations, pursuing invariably the same object, evinces a design to reduce them under absolute despotism, it is their right, it is their duty to throw off such government, and to provide new guards for their future security. Such has been the patient sufferance of these colonies; and such is now the necessity which constrains them to *alter* their former systems of government. The history of the present King of Great Britain is a history of *repeated* injuries and usurpations, *all having* in direct object the establishment of an absolute tyranny over these states. To prove this, let facts be submitted to a candid world. . . .

Jefferson worked on his draft of the Declaration of Independence in his rooms in a house at the corner of Philadelphia's Market and Seventh Streets. That copy still survives, with extensive editing in Jefferson's own hand. Left, Benjamin Franklin, John Adams, Jefferson, and others present the declaration to John Hancock, President of the Congress. During debate on the question of independence, Franklin reminded the assembled colonists of the gravity of their decision. "We must all hang together," he warned, "or most assuredly we shall all hang separately." Painting Yale University, New Haven, CT/A.K.G., Berlin/SuperStock.

He [King George] has waged cruel war against human nature itself, violating its most sacred rights of life and liberty in the persons of a distant people who never offended him, captivating and carrying them into slavery in another hemisphere, or to incur miserable death in their transportation thither. This piratical warfare, the opprobrium of INFIDEL powers, is the warfare of the CHRISTIAN king of Great Britain. Determined to keep open a market where MEN should be bought and sold, he has prostituted his negative for suppressing every legislative attempt to prohibit or to restrain this execrable commerce. And that this assemblage of horrors might want no fact of distinguished die, he is now exciting those very people to rise in arms among us, and to purchase that liberty of which he has deprived them, by murdering the people on whom he also obtruded them: thus paying off former crimes committed against the LIBERTIES of one people, with crimes which he urges them to commit against the LIVES of another.

Thomas Jefferson, from a clause removed from his original draft of the Declaration of Independence

The facts of the actual signing of the Declaration of Independence have been in dispute for more than two hundred years. Historians believe today that only John Hancock, president of the Congress, signed the document on July 4, 1776. For reasons unclear, but perhaps owing to the openly treasonous nature of the declaration and fear of personal reprisals by the British, or perhaps for the simple reason that the final, printed version was not ready until then, Jefferson and the remaining members of the Congress are believed to have signed on August 2. Engraving the National Portrait Gallery, Smithsonian Institution. Photo Art Resource.

This was the object of the Declaration of Independence. Not to find out new principles, or new arguments, never before thought of, not merely to say things that had never been said before; but to place before mankind the common sense of the subject, in terms so plain and firm as to command their assent, and to justify ourselves in the independent stand we are compelled to take. Neither aiming at originality of principle or sentiment, nor yet copied from any particular and previous writing, it was intended to be an expression of the American mind, and to give to that expression the proper tone and spirit called for by the occasion.

Thomas Jefferson, from a letter to Henry Lee, May 8, 1825

AN ACT FOR ESTABLISHING RELIGIOUS FREEDOM

THOMAS JEFFERSON

The Virginia act for religious freedom has been received with infinite approbation in Europe, and propagated with enthusiasm. I do not mean by the governments, but by the individuals who compose them. It has been translated into French and Italian, has been sent to most of the courts of Europe, and has been the best evidence of the falsehood of those reports which stated us to be in anarchy. . . . In fact, it is comfortable to see the standard of reason at length erected, after so many ages, during which the human mind has been held in vassalage by kings, priests, and nobles; and it is honorable for us, to have produced the first legislature who had the courage to declare, that the reason of man may be trusted with the formation of his own opinions.

Thomas Jefferson, from a letter to James Madison, December 16, 1786, after the passage of Jefferson's Act for Establishing Religious Freedom by the Virginia legislature

In September of 1776, with the Declaration of Independence completed and the Revolution in progress, Jefferson gave up his seat in the Continental Congress and returned to Virginia. He was anxious to be with his wife, whose health had been poor, and equally anxious to participate in the formation of the new state government. In Jefferson's mind, it was at the level of the individual states that the new American nation must take shape. He had three main objectives as he began his work in the Virginia legislature: to reform the laws to make land available to all citizens, to provide for quality general education, and to guarantee freedom of religion. On June 13, 1779, John Harvie introduced Jefferson's Act for Establishing Religious Freedom to the Virginia state legislature. The first of its kind in world history, the bill met with strong opposition and would not pass for seven years. At the end of his days, Jefferson counted the statute among the three greatest achievements of his lifetime. Below is Jefferson's text as accepted by the Virginia legislature in 1786.

Well aware that Almighty God hath created the mind free; that all attempts to influence it by temporal punishments or burdens, or by civil incapacitations, tend only to beget habits of hypocrisy and meanness, and are a departure from the plan of the Holy Author of our religion, who being Lord both of body and mind, yet chose not to propagate it by coercions on either, as was in his Almighty power to do; that the impious presumption of legislators and rulers, civil as well as ecclesiastical, who, being themselves but fallible and uninspired men have assumed dominion over the faith of others, setting up their own opinions and modes of thinking as the only true and infallible, and as such endeavoring to impose them on others, hath established and maintained false religions over the greatest part of the world, and through all time; that to compel a man to furnish contributions of money for the propagation of opinions which he disbelieves, is sinful and tyrannical; that even the forcing him to support this or that teacher of his own religious persuasion, is depriving him of the comfortable liberty of giving his contributions to the particular pastor whose morals he would make his pattern, and whose powers he feels most persuasive to righteousness, and is withdrawing from the ministry those temporal rewards, which proceeding from an approbation of their personal conduct, are an additional incitement to earnest and unremitting labors for the instruction of mankind; that our civil rights have no dependence on our religious opinions, more than our opinions in physics or geometry; that, therefore, the proscribing any citizen as unworthy the public confidence by laying upon him an incapacity of being called to the offices of trust and emolument, unless he profess or renounce this or that religious opinion, is depriving him injuriously of those privileges and advantages to which in common with his fellow citizens he has a natural right; that it tends also to corrupt the principles of that very religion it is meant to encourage, by bribing, with a monopoly of worldly honors and emoluments, those who will externally profess and conform to it; that though indeed these are criminal who do not withstand such temptation, yet neither are those innocent who lay the bait in their way; that to suffer the civil magistrate to intrude his powers into the field of opinion and to restrain the profession or propagation of principles, on the supposition of their ill tendency, is a dangerous fallacy, which at once destroys all religious liberty, because he being of course judge of that tendency, will make his opinions the rule of judgment, and approve or condemn the sentiments of others only as they shall square with or differ from his own; that it is time enough for the rightful purposes of civil government, for its offices to interfere when principles break out into overt acts against peace and good order; and finally, that truth is great and will prevail if left to herself, that she is the proper and sufficient antagonist to error, and has nothing to fear from the conflict, unless by human interposition disarmed of her natural weapons, free argument and debate, errors ceasing to be dangerous when it is permitted freely to contradict them.

Be it therefore enacted by the General Assembly, That no man shall be compelled to frequent or support any religious worship, place or ministry whatsoever, nor shall be enforced, restrained, molested, or burthened in his body or goods, nor shall otherwise suffer on account of his religious opinions or belief, but that all men shall be free to profess, and by argument to maintain, their opinions in matters of religion, and that the same shall in nowise diminish, enlarge, or affect their civil capacities.

And though we well know this Assembly, elected by the people for the ordinary purposes of legislation only, have no power to restrain the acts of succeeding assemblies, constituted with the powers equal to our own, and that therefore to declare this act irrevocable, would be of no effect in law, yet we are free to declare, and do declare, that the rights hereby asserted are of the natural rights of mankind, and that if any act shall be hereafter passed to repeal the present or to narrow its operation, such act will be an infringement of natural right.

The error seems not sufficiently eradicated, that the operations of the mind, as well as the acts of the body, are subject to the coercion of the laws. But our rulers can have no authority over such natural rights, only as we have submitted to them. The rights of conscience we never submitted, we could not submit. We are answerable for them to our God. The legitimate powers of government extend to such acts only as are injurious to others. But it does me no injury for my neighbor to say there are twenty gods, or no God. It neither picks my pocket nor breaks my leg. If it be said, his testimony in a court of justice cannot be relied on, reject it then, and be the stigma on him. Constraint may make him worse by making him a hypocrite, but it will never make him a truer man. It may fix him obstinately in his errors, but will not cure them. Reason and free inquiry are the only effectual agents against error. Give a loose to them, they will support the true religion by bringing every false one to their tribunal, to the test of their investigation. They are the natural enemies of error, and of error only. Had not the Roman government permitted free inquiry, Christianity could never have been introduced. . . . Subject opinion to coercion: whom will you make your inquisitors? Fallible men; men governed by bad passions, by private as well as public reasons. And why subject it to coercion? To produce uniformity. But is uniformity of opinion desirable? No more than of face and stature. Introduce the bed of Procrustes then, and as there is danger that the large men may beat the small, make us all of a size, by lopping the former and stretching the latter. Difference of opinion is advantageous in religion. The several sects perform the office of a censor morum over each other. Is uniformity attainable? Millions of innocent men, women, and children, since the introduction of Christianity, have been burnt, tortured, fined, imprisoned; yet we have not advanced one inch towards uniformity.

Thomas Jefferson, from Notes on Virginia

James Madison, who led the movement to pass Jefferson's Act for Establishing Religious Freedom in the Virginia legislature, declared that the document would "extinguish forever the ambitious hope of making laws for the human mind." The statute was widely read and acclaimed throughout Europe, where it was taken as undeniable proof that America was a truly free and enlightened nation. At left, the capitol building in Williamsburg. It was in Williamsburg that Jefferson settled in late 1776 to begin his work on state reforms. In 1789, he would design a capitol building for the new seat of Virginia government, the city of Richmond. Photo SuperStock.

WARTIME GOVERNOR

FROM *JEFFERSON HIMSELF*, BY BERNARD MAYO

Jefferson became governor of Virginia during a time when the British, unable to win the war in the North, had decided to take the fight to the South. Battles raged in Savannah, Augusta, and Charleston, moving ever closer to Jefferson's Virginia, a state whose forces were weak at sea and spread thin over the wild and mountainous land. At the time Jefferson left the governorship, the state was in crisis; if he had served only months longer, he would have presided over the state as the war was ended and the independence he had so eloquently declared was affirmed. General George Washington, below, accepted the British surrender at Yorktown on October 19, 1781. Portrait by Charles Willson Peale, The Huntington Library, Art Collections, and Botanical Gardens, San Marino, CA/SuperStock.

Elected by the General Assembly to the office of governor of Virginia in June of 1779, thirty-six-year-old Jefferson accepted the responsibilities of office with a sense of duty, but little enthusiasm. "In times like these," he wrote to his friend Richard Henry Lee, "public offices are burthens to those appointed to them." The nation was still immersed in its revolutionary battle with Great Britain, and, as governor, Jefferson held little real authority; however, he bore a great burden of responsibility. After two single-year terms, at a moment when the battles of the Revolutionary War were raging throughout Virginia, Jefferson left office amid great turmoil and controversy.

Jefferson was thirty-six, the leader of the democratic forces, when he was elected Governor of Virginia in 1779. His position, especially after his re-election in 1780, was one of exceptional difficulty. From the beginning of the Revolution his state had given generously of troops and supplies to Washington's army in the north. Now, with the British under Lord Cornwallis invading the Carolinas and advancing on Virginia, the young Governor was forced to drain off more men and equipment to the defending army in the south. Further, Virginia's western frontier was menaced by the British and Indians, and her seaboard was not only harassed by British expeditionary forces but successfully invaded by the traitor Benedict Arnold, who penetrated up the James River as far as the new capital of Richmond.

As governor of an invaded and war-exhausted state Jefferson struggled as best he could against tremendous obstacles: the want of arms, money, and essential supplies; the disaffection of the Tories; the dependence upon short-term and untried militia. Virginia's plight became desperate when Cornwallis in May of 1781 effected a junction with Arnold. Opposed only by militia and a small detachment of Continentals under Lafayette, the British ravaged the state with fire and sword during the months preceding their surrender that fall at Yorktown. Jefferson himself, as he tells us, suffered severe property losses, and he came very near being captured when Colonel Tarleton made his famous raid on Charlottesville in June of 1781.

At this crisis, just as his second term was about to expire, he was shocked into angry protest by the clamor for a dictator with unlimited power, the very thought of which was treason against democracy, treason against mankind in general. He keenly resented criticism of his military measures during the invasion, and his resentment continued even after the legislature unanimously and warmly commended his services as war governor.

DISILLUSIONMENT

FROM *THOMAS JEFFERSON AND THE NEW NATION*, BY MERRILL D. PETERSON

After Jefferson's resignation from the governor's office, some members of the legislature, led by Patrick Henry, charged that he had left his office before a successor had been named and thus endangered the people at a time of great crisis. Jefferson eventually stood before the legislature and answered the charges. His name was cleared and an apology issued; but Jefferson, already devastated by the call of some Virginians for a dictatorial governor, was scarred by the experience, and he retired to private life bitter and disillusioned.

His governorship could not be reckoned brilliant or even successful. Yet if faithfulness to duty, courage in distress, calmness and forecast of mind, devotion to republican principles, flexibility in the face of danger, and an enlarged view of Virginia's place in the grand strategy of the Union—if these things were important, then Jefferson was more deserving of praise than of blame. He certainly never claimed more for himself. He knew, and frankly conceded, how far character and training unsuited him to the role of a wartime governor, and he endorsed the assembly's choice of a military commander, General Nelson, to succeed him. But he knew that some circumstances are unyielding, that some evils are mild when compared with the evils likely to result from their suppression, and, as he stated to Lafayette, "that public misfortunes may be produced as well by public poverty and private disobedience to the laws as by the misconduct of public servants."

The panic that accompanied his retirement was unjustified. The government had not collapsed. The assembly was in being, the War Office and other administrative offices continued to function, and the executive was fully restored by the middle of June. The state maintained its independence and the loyalty of its people. Its military strength constantly increased while Cornwallis exhausted himself in useless marches. "Overrunning a Country is not to conquer it," Lafayette wisely observed of the lord commander's movements, adding by way of illustration, "and if it was construed into a right of possession, the French could claim the whole German Empire." Virginia's situation would have been much worse had the executive, bowing to the wishes of Steuben and Greene, stripped the state of all defensive capabilities in the spring. The nucleus of defense remained. Lafayette's force engaged Cornwallis until fresh militia could be mobilized, until Steuben's recruits were diverted from a fruitless march southward and drawn into the field, and until Wayne's army arrived from Pennsylvania. All of this occurred at the time of Jefferson's retirement. By the middle of June, Lafayette's army, now numbering perhaps 8000 men, was superior to the enemy's. The second division of the French fleet, with 24 warships and 3000 troops, lay poised in Caribbean waters. Congress was making every endeavor to aid Virginia. And Washington closely watched the developments there. When Cornwallis, in short order, withdrew his fever-ridden army into Yorktown, the outcome was a military certainty. Going into retirement, Jefferson could not foresee in detail the culmination of this chain of events, but he had never once doubted the ultimate triumph of American arms, and he turned to the long deferred pleasures of private life confident of an early victory and an early peace.

Our circumstances being much distressed, it was proposed . . . to create a dictator, invested with every power legislative, executive, and judiciary, civil and military, of life and of death, over our persons and over our properties; . . . and wanted a few votes only of being passed. One who entered into this contest from a pure love of liberty, and a sense of injured rights, who determined to make every sacrifice, and to meet every danger, for the re-establishment of those rights on a firm basis, who did not mean to expend his blood and substance for the wretched purpose of changing this master for that, but to place the powers of governing him in a plurality of hands of his own choice, so that the corrupt will of no one man might in future oppress him, must stand confounded and dismayed when he is told that a considerable portion of that plurality had meditated the surrender of them into a single hand, and, in lieu of a limited monarch, to deliver him over to a despotic one! . . .

Was it from the necessity of the case? . . . The very thought alone was treason against the people; was treason against mankind in general; as riveting forever the chains which bow down their necks, by giving to their oppressors a proof, which they would have trumpeted through the universe, of the imbecility of republican government, in times of pressing danger, to shield them from harm. Those who assume the right of giving away the reins of government in any case, must be sure that the herd, whom they hand on to the rods and hatchet of the dictator, will lay their necks on the block when he shall nod to them. But if our assemblies supposed such a recognition in the people, I hope they mistook their character.

Thomas Jefferson, from Notes on Virginia

THOMAS AND MARTHA

FROM *IN PURSUIT OF REASON*, BY NOBLE E. CUNNINGHAM

While Jefferson was helping to lead the Revolution, he was also building upon his dream of domestic tranquility at Monticello. Beginning in 1770, the focus of that domestic life was a young widow named Martha Wayles Skelton, who became Jefferson's wife in 1772. Very little is known about the relationship of Jefferson and his wife—he destroyed all his letters to her following her tragic death just ten years after their marriage. What is known from other sources reveals that their life together was a happy one despite its brevity, their frequent separations, and the tragic loss of four children.

At the time he started building his home, Jefferson did not know who would share it with him, but he soon was interrupting his work to visit Martha Wayles Skelton at the Forest, her father's house in Charles City County, near Williamsburg. These visits began in October, 1770, and increased in frequency during 1771. In June of that year Jefferson sent to England for a pianoforte "worthy the acceptance of a lady for whom I intend it," and in August he confided that "in every scheme of happiness she is placed in the fore-ground of the picture, as the principal figure. Take that away, and it is no picture for me." This was Jefferson's first serious romantic attachment since his adolescent love affair with Rebecca Burwell. In the intervening years nothing in the record indicates his being attracted to any women except for an imprudent advance to Betsy Walker, wife of his friend John Walker. Years later he admitted that "when young and single I offered love to a handsome lady," and he acknowledged "its incorrectness." This appears to have been an exceptional circumstance, and until he met Martha Skelton, he seems to have been less interested in women than in establishing himself in law and in politics. During these years he had taken seriously his responsibilities to his mother and to his younger sisters and brother. He had been much shaken in 1765 by the death of his oldest sister, Jane, who was twenty-five and had been particularly close to him. Thus, a number of circumstances may have contributed to what appeared to be a lack of interest in finding a wife. All of this changed when he fell in love with Martha.

Five and a half years younger than Jefferson, Martha Wayles Skelton was the young widow of Bathurst Skelton, whom Jefferson had known while Skelton was a student at William and Mary. The daughter of John Wayles, a prosperous lawyer with a large landed estate, Martha had married Bathurst Skelton when she was eighteen, borne a son at nineteen, and become a widow before she was twenty. It was about two years after this that Jefferson met her, probably in Williamsburg in the autumn of 1770, and soon thereafter began to pay her increasing attention. Indeed, he apparently courted her with all the formality that the word suggests. Within a year she had agreed to marry him, and on the first day of January, 1772, they were married at the Forest. Martha was twenty-three and Jefferson twenty-eight—somewhat older than most Virginia men married in his day. In the summer before their marriage, her son, John Skelton, not yet four, died, and Jefferson never gained the stepson for whom he had already begun to make plans.

No portrait of Martha Wayles Jefferson survives, and the rare contemporary descrip-

tions of her offer few details. Family tradition describes her as beautiful and musically talented. Her brother-in-law Robert Skipwith told Jefferson not long before their marriage that she was a woman "with the greatest fund of good nature" and "all that sprightliness and sensibility which promises to ensure you the greatest happiness mortals are capable of enjoying." No description of Martha in Jefferson's own hand survives, nor any letter between them, for he apparently destroyed such private papers as might have revealed his deepest personal feelings. But there is every reason to believe that he found Skipwith's prediction to be true and that their marriage was a happy one.

There are no portraits of Jefferson at the time of his marriage, and none would be painted until he went to Europe after the Revolution. Nor are there any written descriptions dating from that time. But we know from later descriptions that he was over six feet tall and somewhat lanky; his eyes were hazel, his hair reddish, and he tended to freckle in the sun. Unlike other times of his life, at this period he appears to have been careful about his dress. While courting Martha, he even ordered from London "a large Umbrella with brass ribs covered with green silk, and neatly finished." He had already shown a shyness that he would only gradually overcome and a sensitivity that he would never lose. He was never referred to as handsome, but the impression that he made on others was generally pleasing. As he made his mark in the world, others would more often record these impressions. When he took Martha to Monticello as his wife, neither of them could have anticipated the events that would make him known beyond the Virginia society into which they both had been born and in which they expected to live out their lives.

No portrait exists of Martha Wayles Skelton Jefferson, a woman whose brief life was marked by an inordinate amount of tragedy. "Pleasure is always before us," Jefferson would later write to a friend, "but misfortune is at our side." Such was the life of his beloved wife, who saw four of her seven children die in infancy. Mrs. Jefferson was a quiet woman who loved music. She had a major role in the management of Monticello and kept meticulous records of the plantation's day-to-day affairs. Yet she spent much of her time at Monticello without the company of her husband and must have struggled mightily to manage the house and her children through periods of repeated illness and seemingly unrelenting grief. It is said that on her death bed, Martha asked her husband to save her children the trauma of accepting a stepmother by remaining single; he complied. Above, Monticello as it looked in 1825, when the grandchildren Martha would never know played on the front lawn. Watercolor by Jane Braddick Peticolas, the Thomas Jefferson Memorial Foundation.

LIFE AT MONTICELLO

FROM *JEFFERSON HIMSELF*, BY BERNARD MAYO

1779

TJ is elected to his first term as governor of Virginia.

1779

TJ's Act for Establishing Religious Freedom is introduced into the Virginia legislature by John Harvie on June 13.

1780

The colonial population is estimated at 2,781,000.

1780

TJ is elected to his second consecutive term as governor of Virginia.

1781

TJ narrowly escapes capture as British forces carry out a raid on the city of Charlottesville, only miles from his Monticello home.

1781

Both sides suffer heavy losses at the Battle of Guilford Courthouse in Connecticut.

1781

TJ leaves the governor's office and returns to Monticello amid great controversy.

1781

British General Charles Cornwallis surrenders to George Washington at Yorktown, Virginia on October 19, 1781.

I have here company enough, part of which is very friendly, part well enough disposed, part secretly hostile, and a constant succession of strangers. But this serves only to get rid of life, not to enjoy it. It is in the love of one's family only that heartfelt happiness is known.

Thomas Jefferson, from a letter to his daughter Mary, October 26, 1801

After their marriage on New Year's Day, 1772, Thomas and Martha Jefferson traveled one hundred miles through the winter landscape to reach Monticello, the home they would share during their ten years as husband and wife. Their daughter Martha later recalled her father's story of how the couple had arrived to find the house dark, the fires out, and the servants all in bed for the night. This was not an omen of bad times to come, however. During the next decade, the Jeffersons would find periods of domestic tranquility at Monticello, despite the continual process of building and remodeling, and despite a series of tragic losses.

In spite of the interruptions of law and politics and war, [Jefferson's] private life during these ten years was that of a many-sided young squire, a cultured Virginia gentleman who was an architect, scientific farmer, and literary essayist, an amateur astronomer and a pioneer scholar in meteorology and natural history. The house of classic simplicity and proportions which he designed and built was the first of many architectural creations that profoundly influenced the whole course of American architecture. It was a two-story brick pavilion with wings, entered front and back by columned porticoes, connected with its service buildings by hidden passageways; a house which commanded a magnificent view of the Blue Ridge Mountains to the west, the hamlet of Charlottesville in the valley immediately below, and on the east a stretch of red-clay farmlands which Jefferson called his sea view. Here at his beloved Monticello, with his wife and children, his farms and his books, he spent the happiest years of his life in "philosophic evenings and rural days."

On his mountaintop Jefferson built roundabout walks and terraced gardens, planted domestic and imported trees and seeds, and kept minute records to see whether foreign specimens could be adapted to the American soil and climate, often comparing notes with Philip Mazzei, an Italian gentleman whom he had induced to start a vineyard in the neighborhood. He trained and directed his slaves in the many farming and building operations of a large plantation which was a little community in itself, with its house and field servants, its waving green fields and orchards and pastures, its horses and cattle and poultry, its gristmill and sawmill and workshops. A bold and skillful horseman, he daily mounted one of his Virginia thoroughbreds and rode over his adjoining farms, conferred with his overseers about the tobacco which he sent down the Rivanna River to warehouses on the James for shipment to England, and often stopped at his deer park, where the tame deer eagerly ran up to eat corn out of his hand.

In his library, surrounded by the books which later became the nucleus of the Library of Congress, he read fiction as well as "the learned lumber" of law and history and science, sketched on his drafting board, and carried on his correspondence with scholars and statesmen. He wrote frequently not only to political colleagues with whom during these years he was creating an American nation, but to scientists such as David Rittenhouse, the Philadelphia astronomer, to whom he reported his observations on the great eclipse of 1778. He was fond of saying that Nature had intended him for the tranquil pursuits of science, rather than a public career, for science was his supreme delight. At the same time, as he tells us, music was the favorite passion of his soul, and one of his dreams was to have his own orchestra at Monticello.

When the Chevalier de Chastellux, an accomplished Parisian and scholarly member of the French Academy, visited Jefferson in the spring of 1782, he was impressed by the classic symmetry and elegant taste of Monticello. He was even more impressed and charmed by Mr. Jefferson, "the first American who has consulted the fine arts to know how he should shelter himself from the weather." Chastellux described his host as a tall man not yet forty, with gentle manners, warm heart, and animated mind; a little reserved at first, he noted, but very soon "we were as intimate as if we had passed our whole lives together." On one memorable evening they drank punch and read the poems of Ossian far into the night. Not only poetry but science, politics, and the arts were the topics of "a conversation always varied and interesting . . . , for no object had escaped Mr. Jefferson; and it seemed as if from his youth he had placed his mind, as he had done his house, on an elevated situation, from which he might contemplate the universe."

Among Jefferson's wide interests were fine food and wine, and meals at Monticello—so often shared with guests—displayed his tastes and learning in both areas. Later in life, after spending time in France, Jefferson would grow particularly fond of French cuisine and would even have one of his slaves, James Hemmings, trained by French chefs. It was Jefferson's custom when entertaining guests to dine early and, after the meal and conversation, to retire to his room for reading, study, or correspondence. The French Chevalier de Chastellux was one of many visitors to Monticello during the years that Jefferson and his wife lived there together. A French nobleman who had joined the colonial forces in the Revolutionary War, Chastellux was quite taken with Monticello and its builder. In 1786, Chastellux published a book about his travels in America in which he called Jefferson a "Musician, Draftsman, Astronomer, Natural philosopher, Jurist, and Statesman." Above, Jefferson's dining room at Monticello. Photo Robert C. Lautman/Monticello.

If there is a gratification, which I envy any people in this world, it is to your country its music. This is the favorite passion of my soul, and fortune has cast my lot in a country where it is in a state of deplorable barbarism. From the line of life in which we conjecture you to be, I have for some time lost hope of seeing you here. Should the event prove so, I shall ask your assistance in procuring a substitute, who may be proficient in singing, &, on the Harpsichord. I should be contented to receive such an one two or three years hence; when it is hoped he may come more safely and find here a greater plenty of those useful things which commerce alone can furnish.

The bounds of an American fortune will not admit the indulgence of a domestic band of musicians, yet I have thought that a passion for music might be reconciled with that economy which we are obliged to observe. I retain among my domestic servants a gardener, a weaver, a cabinet-maker, and a stone-cutter, to which I would add a vigneron. In a country where, like yours, music is cultivated and practiced by every class of men, I suppose there might be found persons of these trades who could perform on the French horn, clarinet, or hautboy and bassoon, so that one might have a band of two French horns, two clarinets, two hautboys, and a bassoon, without enlarging their domestic expenses. A certainty of employment for a half dozen years, and at the end of that time, to find them, if they chose, a conveyance to their own country, might induce them to come here at reasonable wages. Without meaning to give you trouble, perhaps it might be practicable for you, in your ordinary intercourse with your people, to find out such men disposed to come to America. Sobriety and good nature would be desirable parts of their characters. If you think such a plan practicable, and will be so kind as to inform me what will be necessary to be done on my part, I will take care that it should be done.

Thomas Jefferson, from a letter to Italian friend John Fabroni, June 8, 1778

JEFFERSON AND THE
NEW AMERICAN NATION
1782–1809

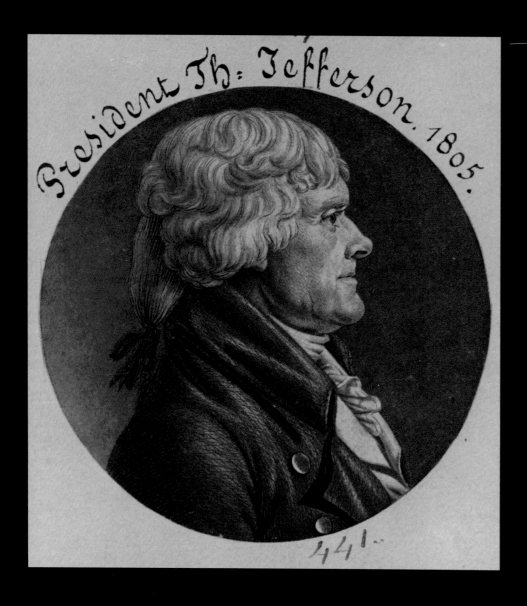

In 1781, after a tumultuous two years as governor of Virginia, Thomas Jefferson retired from public life and returned to Monticello. It was to be only the briefest of respites. In 1782, Jefferson's beloved wife Martha died; later that same year, public duty called him once more, and he emerged from his grief to commit himself to the task of building the new American nation. In the years to come, as the fledgling federal government stretched its wings and tested its limits, Jefferson would emerge as the nation's most powerful voice for the rights of the individual states and of the private citizen. He would witness a revolution in France, correspond with James Madison about the new American Constitution, and serve two terms as president before, nearly three decades after he announced his intention to retire, he finally settled into private life at Monticello.

Portrait, de St. Memin, National Portrait Gallery/Art Resource, NY. President's House, 1826, St. John Baker, Huntington Collection, San Marino, CA/SuperStock.

THE GRIEVING HUSBAND

FROM *IN PURSUIT OF REASON*, BY NOBLE E. CUNNINGHAM

Your letter found me little emerging from the stupor of mind which had rendered me as dead to the world as she whose loss occasioned it. Your letter recalled to my memory that there were persons still living of much value to me. If you should have thought me remiss . . . you will . . . ascribe it to its true cause, the state of dreadful suspense in which I have been kept all the summer, and the catastrophe which closed it.

Thomas Jefferson, from a letter to Francois Jean, Chevalier de Chastellux, November 26, 1782

Martha Jefferson died in September of 1782. Her passing threw Jefferson into a deep and devastating grief. He would never remarry and would speak only rarely of his time together with Martha.

On May 20 Jefferson wrote to Monroe that "Mrs. Jefferson had added another daughter to our family. She has been ever since and still continues very dangerously ill." Martha Jefferson never regained her health, and Jefferson watched helplessly as her life slipped away. Years later his eldest daughter, Martha, who was ten at the time and called Patsy, remembered that her father had constantly attended her mother during this final illness. "For four months that she lingered he was never out of Calling," she recalled. "When not at her bed side he was writing in a small room which opened immediately at the head of her bed." Sometime during her declining months Martha Jefferson copied, with slight modification, from *Tristram Shandy* the poignant lines:

> Time wastes too fast: every letter
> I trace tell me with what rapidity
> life follows my pen. The days and hours
> of it are flying over our heads like
> clouds of windy day never to return—
> more every thing presses on—

This much was in her own hand, but it was left to her devoted husband to complete the passage:

> and every time I kiss thy hand to bid adieu,
> every absence which follows it,
> are preludes to that eternal separation
> which we are shortly to make!

"My history . . . would have been as happy as I could have asked could the objects of my affection have been immortal. But all the favors of fortune have been embittered by domestic losses. Of six children I have lost four, and finally their mother." So wrote Jefferson to his friend Elizabeth Thompson in January 1787, five years after his wife's death. Martha's death marked a turning point in Jefferson's life. Had she not died, in the years to come he may have turned his focus more and more toward family life and building his home at Monticello. With Martha gone, Jefferson sought solace in work, and thus took the path that would eventually lead him to the President's House. At left, Jefferson's bedroom at Monticello, where he remained alone for three weeks after the death of his wife. Photo Robert C. Lautman/Monticello.

When Martha's faltering life came to an end on September 6, 1782, Jefferson's despondency was so intense as to excite the concern of those about him. Years later Patsy recalled: "A moment before the closing scene, he was led from the room in a state of insensibility by his sister, Mrs. Carr, who, with great difficulty, got him into the library, where he fainted, and remained so long insensible that they feared he never would revive." The ten-year-old Patsy was not allowed to witness what followed, but when she sneaked into his room at night, she long remembered her shock at his emotion. Her father stayed in his room three weeks, she recalled. "He walked almost incessantly night and day, only lying down occasionally, when nature was completely exhausted, on a pallet that had been brought in during his long fainting-fit." When at last he left his room, "he was incessantly on horseback, rambling about the mountain, in the least frequented roads, and just as often through the woods." Accompanying him on these "melancholy rambles," the young Patsy found the scenes "beyond the power of time to obliterate."

It was a period of deep depression, and not until mid-October did Jefferson find himself "emerging from that stupor of mind which had rendered me as dead to the world as she was whose loss occasioned it," he admitted in November. By then his friends had rallied to his rescue in an effort to draw him away from the scene of his grief. Prompted by Madison, the delegates to the Continental Congress unanimously voted to renew the appointment earlier offered him as one of the ministers plenipotentiary for negotiating a peace. Jefferson received the news of the appointment on November 25, accepted immediately, and a month later was in Philadelphia waiting for passage to France. "I had folded myself in the arms of retirement, and rested all prospect of future happiness on domestic and literary objects," he wrote to Chastellux on the same day he accepted Congress' commission. "A single event wiped away all my plans and left me a blank which I had not the spirits to fill up." Now Congress had provided him the challenge to fill that void, and he seized it eagerly. The man who had quitted the governor's office in despair eighteen months earlier was back in public service. His life again had meaning.

I am glad to learn that you are employed in things new and good, in your music and drawing. You know what have been my fears for some time past; that you do not employ yourself so closely as I could wish. You have promised me a more assiduous attention, and I have great confidence in what you promise. It is your future happiness which interests me, and nothing can contribute more to it (moral rectitude always excepted) than the contracting a habit of industry and activity. Of all the cankers of human happiness, none corrodes with so silent, yet so baneful a tooth, as indolence. Body and mind both unemployed, our being becomes a burthen, and every object about us loathsome, even the dearest. Idleness begets ennui, ennui the hypochondria, and that a diseased body. No laborious person was ever yet hysterical. Exercise and application produce order in our affairs, health of body, cheerfulness of mind, and these make us precious to our friends. It is while we are young that the habit of industry is formed. If not then, it never is afterwards. The fortune of our lives, therefore, depends on employing well the short period of youth. If at any moment, my dear, you catch yourself in idleness, start from it as you would from the precipice of a gulph.

Thomas Jefferson, from a letter to his daughter Patsy, 1787

Only three of Thomas and Martha Jefferson's six children survived past infancy, and only two—Martha, known as Patsy, and Mary, called Maria and Polly—grew to adulthood. Patsy, born in 1772, closely resembled her father. She lived with Jefferson in Paris from the ages of twelve to seventeen. Later, she married her second cousin Thomas Mann Randolph and often served as Jefferson's hostess while he was president. Polly Jefferson bore more resemblance to her mother than her father. She traveled to France at the age of nine to be with her father and sister after a three-year separation. Polly, who married John Wayles Eppes, died tragically at the age of twenty-five. Jefferson maintained a prolific correspondence with his daughters while they were separated, offering advice, instruction, and encouragement as they grew to maturity. Patsy was ten when her mother died; during her father's intense grief, she was his closest companion. At right, Martha (Patsy) Jefferson Randolph, the Thomas Jefferson Memorial Foundation, photo Edward Owen.

AN AMERICAN ABROAD

THOMAS JEFFERSON, FROM A LETTER TO CHARLES BELLINI, PARIS, 1785

Here the immense extent of uncultivated and fertile land enables every one who will labor, to marry young, and to raise a family of any size. Our food, then, may increase geometrically with our laborers, and our births, however multiplied, become effective.

Thomas Jefferson, comparing American economy to European economy, in a letter to French economist Jean Baptiste Say, February 1, 1804

Martha's death shattered Jefferson's dreams of domestic peace at Monticello. When he finally emerged from his deep grief, he looked away from his mountain for purpose and found himself once again in public service. An appointment as minster to France fell though, but by the end of 1782 he was serving in the Congress, and two years later he was on his way to France as minister plenipotentiary to Europe. He sailed from Boston on July 5, 1784, and arrived in France on July 31. It would be five years before Jefferson returned to American soil. As part of a team that included John Adams and Benjamin Franklin, he was charged with negotiating treaties to improve American commerce and strengthen the young nation. In 1785, Jefferson succeeded the retiring Franklin as American minister to France. The letter excerpted below proves that Jefferson's time in France only strengthened his belief in the importance of building an American government that would safeguard the blessings of the land and the unique freedoms of the people.

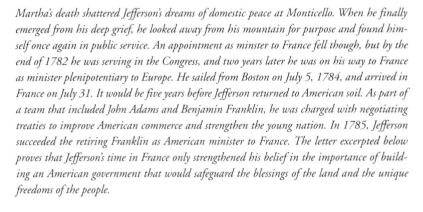

Behold me at length on the vaunted scene of Europe! It is not necessary for your information, that I should enter into details concerning it. But you are, perhaps, curious to know how this new scene has struck a savage of the mountains of America. Not advantageously, I assure you. I find the general fate of humanity here most deplorable. The truth of Voltaire's observation offers itself perpetually, that every man here must be either the hammer or the anvil. It is a true picture of that country to which they say we shall pass hereafter, and where we are to see God and his angels in splendor, and crowds of the damned trampled under their feet.

While the great mass of the people are thus suffering under physical and moral oppression, . . . intrigues of love occupy the younger, and those of ambition, the elder part of the great. Conjugal love having no existence among them, domestic happiness, of which that is the basis, is utterly unknown. In lieu of this, are substituted pursuits which nourish and invigorate all our bad passions, and which offer only moments of ecstasy, amidst days and months of restlessness and torment. Much, very much inferior, this, to the tranquil, permanent felicity with which domestic society in America blesses most of its inhabitants; leaving them to follow steadily those pursuits which health and reason approve, and rendering truly delicious the intervals of those pursuits.

"My God! how little do my countrymen know what precious blessings they are in possession of, and which no other people on earth enjoy. I confess I had no idea of it myself. While we shall see multiplied instances of Europeans going to live in America, I will venture to say, no man now living will ever see an instance of an American removing to settle in Europe, and continuing there." So wrote Jefferson to Madison from Paris in 1785. Along with a deepened appreciation for life in America, Jefferson's time in France provided him with the invaluable opportunity to work with Benjamin Franklin. Franklin was beloved in America and admired throughout the world. When he died in 1790, more than twenty thousand citizens attended his funeral in Philadelphia. Portrait of Franklin by Louis Carrogis de Carmontelle, National Portrait Gallery, Smithsonian Institution/Art Resource.

Jefferson's *Notes on the State of Virginia*

From *In Pursuit of Reason*, by Noble E. Cunningham

While Jefferson was governor of Virginia, he received a query from the Marquis de Barbé-Marbois, a French official in Philadelphia, as to the particular customs, geography, resources, laws, and religious practices of Virginia. Jefferson made notes in response, but it was not until after he left office and retired to Monticello that he transformed these notes into a manuscript, which he sent to Marbois in December of 1781. While he was in Paris, Jefferson published the manuscript under the title Notes on the State of Virginia. *The book was read throughout Europe and became recognized as one of the most important scientific works yet written by an American.* Notes on Virginia *displayed Jefferson's wide range of interests and the incredible breadth of his intelligence. It was especially important in France, where leaders of the coming revolution seized upon its statements concerning the natural rights of man.*

The commentaries in the *Notes on the State of Virginia*, as Jefferson modestly insisted, were incomplete, and some topics were treated far more extensively than others. Although most of the work centered on Virginia, Jefferson ranged far beyond his own state on certain subjects, such as the aborigines and the animals in the New World. When he cited men of genius that America had produced, he pointed to Washington, Franklin, and Rittenhouse, only one of whom was a Virginian. Much of the work was descriptive, factual data about Virginia. He began by describing its boundaries and rivers, providing an amazing amount of information about the waters that flowed through Virginia or along its borders, including the Mississippi. In treating that channel of the future commerce of the western country, he also included its principal source, the Missouri. Even in largely descriptive passages he added opinion, calling the Ohio "the most beautiful river on earth"— a verdict that he had gleaned from others, for he had never seen it himself.

His chapter "Productions Mineral, Vegetable and Animal," the longest in the book, displayed the Virginian's keen interest in natural history and included detailed lists of trees, plants, animals, and birds. The most extensive part of the chapter was Jefferson's argument refuting the theory of the Comte de Buffon, probably the best known and most widely respected naturalist of his day, that the animals and aborigines of the New World were smaller and generally degenerate in comparison with their European equivalents. To provide data, he had friends everywhere measuring and weighing animals, large and small. Jefferson himself was not innovative as a scientist, always valuing the practical over the theoretical, but his section on natural history attracted considerable notice, and throughout his life he would be unexcelled as a promoter of science.

The second-longest section of the book was devoted to the constitution and the laws of Virginia, in which he sharply criticized the Virginia Constitution of 1776. Noting that it "was formed when we were new and unexperienced in the science of government," he was critical of the denial of the franchise to a large number of freemen and also of the unequal representation of the central and western portions of the state in comparison with the old tidewater counties. In addition, he opposed the consolidation of power in the hands of a single branch of government, even the legislature. The concentration of the executive, legislative,

Jefferson's Notes on Virginia *expressed his abiding love of the natural beauty of his native state. In a section on the Natural Bridge, a striking rock arch carved by water in Virginia's mountains, his language soars: "It is impossible for the emotions arising from the sublime to be felt beyond what they are here; so beautiful an arch, so elevated, so light, and springing as it were up to heaven! The rapture of the spectator is really indescribable!" So enamored was Jefferson of the Natural Bridge, in fact, that in 1774, he bought it, along with 157 surrounding acres. Above, a nineteenth-century engraving of the Natural Bridge by J. C. Stadler. Engraving the Thomas Jefferson Memorial Foundation.*

The Virginia legislature, with the support of TJ, enacts a law enabling Virginians to free their slaves through their wills.

1782

TJ's wife, Martha Wayles Skelton Jefferson, dies at Monticello.

1782

The Continental Congress appoints TJ minister to France; the appointment is later rescinded due to changing international relations.

1782

TJ is elected to the Continental Congress.

1783

American ministers sign peace treaty with Great Britain in Paris, formally ending the American Revolution and recognizing American independence.

1783

The first daily newspaper in America begins publication in Philadelphia.

1783

Massachusetts declares slavery a violation of its state constitution.

1783

In December, George Washington resigns as commander of the Continental Army.

and judicial powers of government in the same hands was "precisely the definition of despotic government," he wrote. "It will be no alleviation that these powers will be exercised by a plurality of hands, and not by a single one."

Jefferson devoted a chapter to the American aborigines, and in response to Buffon he argued that "we shall probably find that they are formed in mind as well as in body, on the same module with the 'Homo sapiens Europaeus.'" In a section on laws he discussed slavery and the black race, expressing both his strong condemnation of slavery and his suspicion that blacks were not intellectually equal to whites. He also used most of a brief chapter on manners to describe the effects of slavery on slaveholders. One of the most famous passages of the book was found in a section on manufactures, devoted largely to glorifying agriculture as superior to manufacturing.

> Those who labour in the earth are the chosen people of God, if ever he had a chosen people, whose breasts he has made his peculiar deposit for substantial and genuine virtue. . . . While we have land to labour then, let us never wish to see our citizens occupied at a work-bench, or twirling a distaff. Carpenters, masons, smiths, are wanting in husbandry: but, for the general operations of manufacture, let our workshops remain in Europe. . . . The mobs of great cities add just so much to the support of pure government, as sores do to the strength of the human body. It is the manners and spirit of a people which preserve a republic in vigour.

No brief examination of the work can adequately display the erudition of the author or convey the scope of the analytical and speculative content of the book. Throughout it revealed Jefferson's intense interest in the environment and in natural history, his passionate concern for government and the laws, and his committed involvement in the new society in which he lived. Just before its publication, Charles Thomson urged him to give the book a broader title and pronounced it "a most excellent Natural history not merely of Virginia but of North America and possibly equal if not superior to that of any Country yet published."

FROM *NOTES ON THE STATE OF VIRGINIA*

BY THOMAS JEFFERSON

John Adams, writing about Jefferson's Notes on Virginia, *declared that "the passages upon slavery are worth diamonds." For a man whose feelings on the issue of slavery reflected the conflicting influences of his education and his native Virginia culture, Jefferson spoke eloquently in favor of abolition in the* Notes. *Yet his impassioned statements must be read in the context of his own life—Jefferson himself owned slaves and, despite positions of great power in his lifetime, did little work of practical value toward achieving abolition.*

It is difficult to determine on the standard by which the manners of a nation may be tried, whether *catholic* or *particular.* It is more difficult for a native to bring to that standard the manners of his own nation, familiarized to him by habit. There must doubtless be an unhappy influence on the manners of our people produced by the existence of slavery among us. The whole commerce between master and slave is a perpetual exercise of the most boisterous passions, the most unremitting despotism on the one part, and degrading submissions on the other. Our children see this, and learn to imitate it; for man is an imitative animal. This quality is the germ of all education in him. From his cradle to his grave he is learning to do what he sees others do. If a parent could find no motive either in his philanthropy or his self-love, for restraining the intemperance of passion towards his slave, it should always be a sufficient one that his child is present. But generally it is not sufficient, The parent storms, the child looks on, catches the lineaments of wrath, puts on the same airs in the circle of smaller slaves, gives a loose to the worst of passions, and thus nursed, educated, and daily exercised in tyranny, cannot but be stamped by it with odious peculiarities. The man must be a prodigy who can retain his manners and morals undepraved by such circumstances. And with what execration should the statesman be loaded, who, permitting one half the citizens thus to trample on the rights of the other, transforms those into despots, and these into enemies, destroys the morals of the one part, and the *amor patriae* of the other. For if a slave can have a country in this world, it must be any other in preference to that in which he is born to live and labor for another; in which he must lock up the faculties of his nature, contribute as far as depends on his individual endeavors to the evanishment of the human race, or entail his own miserable condition on the endless generations proceeding from him. With the morals of the people, their industry also is destroyed. For in a warm climate, no man will labor for himself who can make another labor for him. This is so true, that of the proprietors of slaves a very small proportion indeed are ever seen to labor. And can the liberties of a nation be thought secure when we have removed their only firm basis, a conviction in the minds of the people that these liberties are of the gift of God? That they are not to be violated but with His wrath? Indeed I tremble for my country when I reflect that God is just; that his justice cannot sleep forever; that considering numbers, nature and natural means only, a revolution of the wheel of fortune, an exchange of situation is among possible events; that it may become probably by supernatural interference! The Almighty has no attribute which can take side with us in such a contest. But it is impossible to be temperate and to pursue this subject through the various considerations of policy, of morals, of history natural and civil. We must be contented to hope they will force their way into every one's mind. I think a change already perceptible, since the origin of the present revolution. The spirit of the master is abating, that of the slave rising from the dust, his condition mollifying, the way I hope preparing, under the auspices of heaven, for a total emancipation, and that this is disposed, in the order of events, to be with the consent of the masters, rather than by their extirpation.

Plantations and slave labor dominated the American South during Jefferson's time. Jefferson has been criticized by students of American history who see only hypocrisy in his public belief in the natural rights of man and his private ownership of slaves. Jefferson himself was not unaware of the conflict between his public statements and his private actions, and to his credit he did make several attempts to move the country toward a legal ban on slavery. In 1784, he included a clause banning slavery in his Report on Government for the Western Territories. When the clause was stricken by a narrow vote, he reacted with anger and foreboding, writing to a friend, "The voice of a single individual . . . would have prevented this abominable crime from spreading itself over the new country. Thus we see the fate of millions unborn hanging on the tongue of one man, and Heaven was silent in that awful moment! But it is to be hoped it will not always be silent, and that the friends to the rights of human nature will in the end prevail."

THE NEW CONSTITUTION

THOMAS JEFFERSON, FROM A LETTER TO JAMES MADISON, DECEMBER 20, 1787

1784

TJ is appointed minister plenipotentiary to Europe.

1784

A major depression cripples the American economy; conditions will not improve until 1788.

1785

TJ succeeds Benjamin Franklin as minister to France on March 10.

1785

The New York legislature passes an act providing for the gradual emancipation of slaves in the state. New Jersey will pass similar legislation the following year.

1785

Regular stage coach routes are established to link New York City, Boston, Albany, and Philadelphia.

1786

Shay's Rebellion begins in Massachusetts as farmers revolt against national economic policies; TJ praises the rebellion as proof of the vitality of the nation.

1787

The Constitutional Convention meets in Philadelphia to begin revising the Articles of Confederation.

1787

Delegates reach agreement on the Constitution on September 17 and submit the document to the states for ratification.

Tho' written constitutions may be violated in moments of passion or delusion, yet they furnish a text to which those who are watchful may again rally and recall the people; they fix too for the people the principles for their political creed.

Thomas Jefferson, from a letter to Joseph Priestly, June 19, 1802

In 1776, when his home state of Virginia adopted its new constitution, Jefferson was in Philadelphia serving in the Continental Congress; he deeply regretted the missed opportunity to help define the fundamental laws of his native state. In 1787, Jefferson missed out again; as American delegates met in Philadelphia to draft a constitution for the new nation, Jefferson was in Paris, cut off from the debate by an ocean and the tedious pace of the mail. He and James Madison corresponded at length about the new Constitution, but it was Madison, not Jefferson, who was in Philadelphia and at the center of the document's creation. Their lengthy correspondence, delayed weeks at a time by the mail, was of little real use in the actual framing of the Constitution. Still, it is of great interest to historians and reveals the depth of Jefferson's desire to protect the freedoms of the American people.

I like very much the general idea of framing a government, which should go on of itself, peaceably, without needing continual recurrence to the State legislatures. I like the organization of the government into legislative, judiciary and executive. I like the power given the legislature to levy taxes, and for that reason solely, I approve of the greater House being chosen by the people directly. For though I think a House so chosen, will be very far inferior to the present Congress, will be very illy qualified to legislate for the Union, for foreign nations, etc., yet this evil does not weigh against the good, of preserving inviolate the fundamental principle, that the people are not to be taxed but by representatives chosen immediately by themselves. I am captivated by the compromise of the opposite claims of the great and little States, of the latter to equal, and the former to proportional influence. I am much pleased, too, with the substitution of the method of voting by person, instead of that of voting by States; and I like the negative given to the Executive, conjointly with a third of either House; though I should have liked it better, had the judiciary been associated for that purpose, or invested separately with a similar power. There are other good things of less moment. I will now tell you what I do not like. First, the omission of a bill of rights, providing clearly, and without the aid of sophism, for freedom of religion, freedom of the press, protection against standing armies, restriction of monopolies, the eternal and unremitting force of the habeas corpus laws, and trials by jury in all matters of fact triable by the laws of the land, and not by the laws of nations. To say, as Mr. Wilson does, that a bill of rights was not necessary, because all is reserved in the case of the general government which is not given, while in the particular ones, all is given which is not reserved, might do for the audience to which it was addressed; but it is surely a *gratis dictum*, the reverse of which might just as well be said; and it is opposed by strong inferences from the body of the instrument, as well as from the omission of the cause of our present Confederation, which had made the reservation in express terms. . . . Let me add, that a bill of rights is what the people are entitled to against every government on earth, general or particular; and what no just government should refuse, or rest on inference.

The second feature I dislike, and strongly dislike, is the abandonment, in every instance, of the principle of rotation in office, and most particularly in the case of the President. Reason and experience tell us, that the first magistrate will always be re-elected if he may be re-elected. He is then an officer for life. This once observed, it becomes of so much consequence to certain nations to have a friend or a foe at the head of our affairs, that they will interfere with money and with arms. A Galloman, or an Angloman, will be supported by the nation he befriends. If once elected, and at a second or third election out-voted by one or two votes, he will pretend false votes, foul play, hold possession of the reins of government, be supported by the States voting for him, especially if they be the central ones, lying in a compact body themselves, and separating their opponents; and they will be aided by one nation in Europe, while the majority are aided by another. The election of a President of America, some years hence, will be much more interesting to certain nations of Europe, than ever the election of a King of Poland was. Reflect on all the instances in history, ancient and modern, of elective monarchies, and say if they do not give foundation for my fears; the Roman Emperors, the Popes while they were of any importance, the German Emperors till they became hereditary in practice, the Kings of Poland, the Deys of the Ottoman dependencies. It may be said, that if elections are to be attended with these disorders, the less frequently they are repeated the better. But experience says, that to free them from disorder, they must be rendered less interesting by a necessity of change. No foreign power, nor domestic party, will waste their blood and money to elect a person, who must go out at the end of a short period. . . .

This is what might be said, and would probably produce a speedy, more perfect and more permanent form of government. At all events, I hope you will not be discouraged from making other trials, if the present one should fail. We are never permitted to despair of the commonwealth. I have thus told you freely what I like, and what I dislike, merely as a matter of curiosity; for I know it is not in my power to offer matter of information to your judgment, which has been formed after hearing and weighing everything which the wisdom of man could offer on these subjects. I own, I am not a friend to a very energetic government. It is always oppressive. It places the governors indeed more at their ease, at the expense of the people. The late rebellion in Massachusetts has given more alarm, than I think it should have done. Calculate that one rebellion in thirteen States in the course of eleven years, is but one for each State in a century and a half. No country should be so long without one. Nor will any degree of power in the hands of government, prevent insurrections. In England, where the hand of power is heavier than with us, there are seldom half a dozen years without an insurrection. In France, where it is still heavier, but less despotic, as Montesquieu supposes, than in some other countries, and where there are always two or three hundred thousand men ready to crush insurrections, there have been three in the course of the three years I have been here, in every one of which greater numbers were engaged than in Massachusetts, and a great deal more blood was spilt. . . . Compare again the ferocious

Jefferson met James Madison in 1776, when he and the then twenty-five-year-old fellow Virginian served on the committee on religion in the Virginia House of Delegates. While Jefferson was in France, Madison pushed his friend's statute on religious freedom through the Virginia legislature, and also, in a series of lengthy letters, sought his opinion on the framing of the new American Constitution. In a letter written to Madison shortly before his own death in 1826, Jefferson wrote, "the friendship which has subsisted between us, now half a century, and the harmony of our political principles and pursuits, have been sources of constant happiness to me throughout that long period." Above, a portrait of James Madison by Chester Harding, National Portrait Gallery, Smithsonian Institution/Art Resource, NY.

A bill of rights is what the people are entitled to against every government on earth, general or particular; and what no just government should refuse, or rest on inferences.

Thomas Jefferson, from a letter to James Madison, December 20, 1787

1787–1789
TJ, in France, corresponds with James Madison about the drafting of the new Constitution.

1787
Publication of the series of essays known as The Federalist begins. In all, eighty-five essays on the questions raised during the debate over the new Constitution will be written by Alexander Hamilton, James Madison, and John Jay.

1787
The Northwest Ordinance establishes the Northwest Territory, providing for government, outlining statehood procedures, and banning slavery in the territory.

1788
New York City is declared the temporary American capital.

1788
New Hampshire becomes the ninth state to ratify the United States Constitution in June, guaranteeing its adoption.

1789
The first session of the United States Congress convenes on March 4.

1789
On March 4, the United States Constitution is declared effective.

1789
The Marquis de Lafayette seeks input from TJ on the French Declaration of the Rights of Man as France moves closer to revolution.

depredations of their insurgents, with the order, the moderation and the almost self-extinguishment of ours. And say, finally, whether peace is best preserved by giving energy to the government, or information to the people. This last is the most certain, and the most legitimate engine of government. Educate and inform the whole mass of the people. Enable them to see that it is their interest to preserve peace and order, and they will preserve them. And it requires no very high degree of education to convince them of this. They are the only sure reliance for the preservation of our liberty. After all, it is my principle that the will of the majority should prevail. If they approve the proposed constitution in all its parts, I shall concur in it cheerfully, in hopes they will amend it, whenever they shall find it works wrong. . . . I have tired you by this time with disquisitions which you have already heard repeated by others a thousand and a thousand times; and therefore, shall only add assurances of the esteem and attachment with which I have the honor to be, dear Sir, your affectionate friend and servant.

In the earliest years of independence, America was governed by the Articles of Confederation, which went into effect in 1781. But the Articles proved inadequate to the task of governing the nation, and on May 25, 1787, a Constitutional Convention was convened in the city of Philadelphia to amend the Articles of Confederation. The result of this convention would be an entirely new document, the United States Constitution. While Jefferson remained in France, fulfilling his duties as minister, the members of the Constitutional Convention fiercely debated the future of the new nation. They submitted the resulting document to the states for ratification on September 17, 1787. Above, a view of the High Street in Philadelphia, circa 1799, the Thomas Jefferson Memorial Foundation.

JEFFERSON AND THE BILL OF RIGHTS

THOMAS JEFFERSON, FROM A LETTER TO JAMES MADISON, JULY 31, 1788

Jefferson was pleased when the new Constitution was finally accepted, but he remained insistent that the document needed a formal bill of rights. The opposing argument held that a written statement of rights was not necessary because the federal government was being granted only a very specific number of powers; the argument also held that the built-in system of checks and balances would provide ample protection for the people. Jefferson insisted, however, that the people's fundamental rights must not be assumed, but guaranteed in writing. Eventually, they were, in the form of the first ten amendments to the Constitution, adopted by Congress on December 15, 1791. Below, Jefferson argues his ideas to Madison in a letter from Paris.

I sincerely rejoice at the acceptance of our new constitution by nine States. It is a good canvas, on which some strokes only want retouching. What these are, I think are sufficiently manifested by the general voice from north to south, which calls for a bill of rights. It seems pretty generally understood, that this should go to juries, habeas corpus, standing armies, printing, religion and monopolies. I conceive there may be difficulty in finding general modifications of these, suited to the habits of all the States. But if such cannot be found, then it is better to establish trials by jury, the right of habeas corpus, freedom of the press and freedom of religion, in all cases, and to abolish standing armies in time of peace, and monopolies in all cases, than not to do it in any. The few cases wherein these things may do evil, cannot be weighed against the multitude wherein the want of them will do evil. . . . A declaration, that the federal government will never restrain the presses from printing anything they please, will not take away the liability of the printers for false facts printed. The declaration, that religious faith shall be unpunished, does not give impunity to criminal acts, dictated by religious error. The saying there shall be no monopolies, lessens the incitements to ingenuity, which is spurred on by the hope of a monopoly for a limited time, as of fourteen years; but the benefit of even limited monopolies is too doubtful, to be opposed to that of their general suppression. If no check can be found to keep the number of standing troops within safe bounds, while they are tolerated as far as necessary, abandon them altogether, discipline well the militia, and guard the magazines with them. More than magazine guards will be useless, if few, and dangerous, if many. No European nation can ever send against us such a regular army as we need fear, and it is hard, if our militia are not equal to those of Canada or Florida. My idea then, is, that though proper exceptions to these general rules are desirable, and probably practicable, yet if the exceptions cannot be agreed on, the establishment of the rules, in all cases, will do ill in very few. I hope, therefore, a bill of rights will be formed, to guard the people against the federal government.

I had intended to have written to your excellency on the subject of the new constitution, but I have already spun out my letter to an immoderate length. I will just observe therefore that according to my ideas there is a great deal of good in it. There are two things however which I dislike strongly. 1. The want of a declaration of rights. I am in hopes the opposition of Virginia will remedy this, and produce such a declaration. 2. The perpetual re-eligibility of the president. This I fear will make an office for life first, and then heredity. I was much an enemy to monarchy before I came to Europe. I am ten thousand times more so since I have seen what they are. There is scarcely an evil known in these countries which may not be traced to their king as its source, nor a good which is not derived from the small fibres of republicanism existing among them. I can further say with safety there is not a crowned head in Europe whose talents or merits would entitle him to be elected a vestryman by the people of any parish in America. However, I shall hope that before there is danger of this change taking place in the office of President, the good sense and free spirit of our countrymen will make the changes necessary to prevent it. Under this hope I look forward to the general adoption of the new constitution with anxiety, as necessary for us under our present circumstances.

Thomas Jefferson, from a letter to George Washington, May 2, 1788

The Earth Belongs to the Living

FROM *JEFFERSON AND THE RIGHTS OF MAN*, BY DUMAS MALONE

1789

French revolutionaries storm the Bastille in Paris. The French Revolution begins. TJ prepares to leave Paris.

1789

George Washington is elected the first president of the United States, with John Adams as vice president.

1789

Washington appoints TJ secretary of state.

1789

Alexander Hamilton is named first secretary of the treasury.

1789

The new Virginia capitol is built in the city of Richmond, as planned by TJ, in a classical revival style.

1790

A Quaker group submits the first emancipation petition to the U.S. Congress.

1790

The American capital is moved from New York to Philadelphia.

1790

The United States Supreme Court holds its first session.

1790

The first American census counts the population at 3,929,625. The count includes 697,624 slaves and 59,557 free blacks. Virginia is the most populous state, with 747,610 citizens.

1790

TJ arrives in Philadelphia in March to begin service as secretary of state.

1790

The federal Naturalization Act establishes a requirement of two years' residence for citizenship.

Jefferson was denied an active role in shaping the American Constitution. Yet his opinion mattered—it was sought by many, manipulated by some, and has been debated for two centuries. Jefferson had his early doubts about the document, but in the end he was firmly, if not blindly, behind it as the best possible protection of the natural rights of Americans.

In later years a common line of partisan attack on Jefferson was that he was in reality a foe to the Constitution. This contention may be dismissed as groundless, though he had a perfect right to oppose it before it was adopted and to criticize it afterwards if he wanted to. His attitude was entirely clear to Madison and Washington, at least, and he has left to posterity a full and candid account of its development. It is wholly incorrect to say, as has been said, that no one knew just how he stood on the fundamental question of the hour when he arrived in Virginia late in 1789, for these leaders did know, and he could not be quoted on both sides except in defiance of chronology. Early in 1789 he wrote to a liberal Englishman: "I did not at first believe that eleven states out of thirteen would have consented to a plan consolidating them as much into one. A change in their dispositions, which had taken place since I left them, had rendered this consolidation necessary, that is to say, had called for a federal government which could walk on its own legs, without leaning for support on the State legislatures." He raised no objections on particularistic grounds, and he found in these events a new and comforting proof that a well informed people could be trusted to remedy their own government, when the need was manifest. Far from regarding the establishment of a new and stronger government as a *coup d'état*, effected for ulterior economic motives by a governing class in defiance of the popular will, he was specially pleased by the unexpected degree of popular support and with the sanity of the procedure. Uneasy France and despotic Europe should learn another lesson from the intelligent processes of a self-governing society. "The example of changing a constitution by assembling the wise men of the State, instead of assembling armies," he said a little later, "will be worth as much to the world as the former examples we had given them." And he regarded the Constitution itself, despite the defects which he continued to point out, as "unquestionably the wisest ever yet presented to men."

Thus he wrote to men of varying political complexion, but, in view of earlier private letters which had been passed around and the unauthorized use of them made by Patrick Henry and others, many of Jefferson's compatriots may have been uncertain of his position during the months before he came home. He must have been designated as an "anti-federalist" by some people, for he wrote a rather elaborate letter because of one report of the sort. His statement of his position in this letter is so colorful that it has lent itself to quotation. It began with an expression of modesty which was in character with the gentleman, and it maintained a balance which may characterize consummate politicians but is unquestionably akin to that of scholars and philosophers:

. . . My opinion was never worthy enough of notice to merit citing; but since you ask it I will tell you. I am not a Federalist, because I never submitted the whole system of my opinions to the creed of any party of men whatever in religion, in philosophy, in politics, or in anything else where I was capable of thinking for myself. Such an addiction is the last degradation of a free and moral agent. If I could not go to heaven but with a party, I would not go there at all. Therefore I protest to you that I am not of the party of federalists. But I am much farther from that of the Antifederalists.

He then traced the development of his attitude to the Constitution, as he did in so many other places, stating that he had always approved the great mass of what was in it, including the "consolidation of the government," but that he still adhered to his two major points of disapproval. One of these he expected would soon be removed, and the other would need to be after Washington had established the new government against the efforts of opposition.

He was of neither party, he said, "nor yet a trimmer between parties." By "parties" he probably meant factional groupings, which he had always steered clear of and which he especially sought to avoid while he was a representative abroad. But the best way to translate his words into modern language is to say that he refused to let his political views be tagged or labeled; he would not let himself be put in any convenient compartment or pigeonhole. No real thinker could ever do that. As to the Constitution and the new government, he sincerely accepted the *fait accompli*, but as a champion of liberty and self-government he intended to maintain his vigilance. The greatest dangers were not immediate but lay ahead.

It was an admirable platform for a philosopher to sit on, and it turned out to be also an excellent political platform. Through force of circumstances, he was freer than most of the leading Americans of his time to heed the voice of popular opinion, and later events showed him to be more disposed than many to do so. Yet he gave no sign of strong personal ambition, and his devoted patriotism may be assumed.

Before he returned to America he gave much thought to the question, whether one generation has the right to bind another, and emerged with the idea that no society has the right to make a perpetual constitution or even a perpetual law. The stimulus came from the discussions then going on in France, and the long letter in which he set forth his speculations to Madison was directed to questions of public debt, which Madison was then considering as a member of Congress. Starting with what he regarded as an axiom of natural law, "that the earth belongs in usufruct to the living," and making elaborate calculations on the life expectancy of such persons as had attained maturity, he arrived at this startling conclusion: "Every constitution, then, and every law, naturally expires at the end of 19 years. If it be enforced longer, it is an act of force and not of right." Madison's perspicuous mind detected flaws in the logic and as a constitution-maker he pointed out grave dangers which would attend periodical revisions of the laws, but he thought the general principle useful and the idea itself a great one. He had long engaged in the practice of correcting the theoretical speculations which emanated from a more daring mind, and was himself immensely stimulated in the process. The most important thing to note here, however, is Jefferson's saying: *The earth belongs always to the living generation.* Believing that, he could be no idolater of any constitution. His genius was not merely that of freedom and reasonableness. It was also the genius of experiment and change.

Although history can be quoted to support any cause, just as scripture can be quoted by the devil, no wrenching of the past can alter a transcending fact about Thomas Jefferson: he believed in the right and capacity of the ordinary man to live responsibly in freedom. Lincoln testified for the ages that the principles of Jefferson were "the definitions and axioms of free society." It is Jefferson, if not Lincoln himself, who is the central figure in the history of American democracy. He fervently believed that the will and welfare of the people were the only prop and purpose of government. Others pitted liberty and equality against each other as if a tension, even a contradiction, existed between them. To Jefferson liberty and equality were complementary qualities of the condition to which man had a moral right. . . .

Jefferson's principles sprang from the deepest aspirations of the people. A communion of sentiment tied him to them, despite his tendency to shrink from too close a personal contact. He expressed himself in literary utterance that was a model of clarity and beauty—understandable, appealing, and almost unfailingly humane. With crisp eloquence he memorably voiced the noblest hopes for human fortune on earth. In so doing, he somehow illuminated the lives of his compatriots—their needs, their best values, their ambitions. His deepest sympathies belonged to the disadvantaged and downtrodden; his deepest trust was in the power of his fellow men to do justice and to fulfill themselves on their own terms, self-reliant and self-governing, as long as they had the opportunity to make informed, unfettered choices; his deepest faith was in the emancipating effect of education and freedom on the human personality. His confidence in popular government, bounded only by respect for minority rights, was anchored in a belief that counting heads was a much better way to rule than breaking them. It secured sounder policies, more beneficial to the general welfare, than those determined by the privileged few.

Leonard W. Levy, from Constitutional Opinions:
Aspects of a Bill of Rights

EYEWITNESS TO A REVOLUTION

FROM *JEFFERSON AND THE RIGHTS OF MAN*, BY DUMAS MALONE

1790

Benjamin Franklin dies in Philadelphia at the age of eighty-four.

1791

The Bill of Rights—comprised of the first ten amendments to the Constitution—goes into effect on December 15.

1791

Thomas Paine publishes The Rights of Man *in England, attacking the monarchy and supporting the causes of the French Revolution. Paine is accused of treason by the British.*

1792

Construction begins on the new U.S. Capitol and the President's House in Washington, D.C.

1792

Two political parties emerge in the United States: the Federalist and the Republican.

1792

George Washington is reelected president on December 5.

1793

Great Britain and France enter into war.

1793

President Washington issues a proclamation of neutrality urging Americans to avoid involvement in the war between Great Britain and France.

1793

The invention of the cotton gin greatly increases cotton production—and the need for slave labor—in the American South.

1793

John Woolman's A Word of Remembrance and Caution to the Rich *is published. The Quaker's pamphlet calls for the abolition of slavery in the United States.*

The summer of 1789 brought revolution to France and found Jefferson—only months away from his return to the United States—very much at the center of the ideological battle in Paris. As a minister of a foreign government, Jefferson was officially neutral, but his heart was with the revolutionaries, whose cause took up the ideals of the American Revolution. Jefferson's influence on the French Revolution was ideological, of course, but also practical. In the summer of 1789, Jefferson's friend the Marquis de Lafayette asked his input on a draft of a document he was preparing for the French National Assembly. That document was A Declaration of the Rights of Man, the French bill of rights, and, as Dumas Malone describes, the finished product showed the hand of the American minister.

In this period of lull before the storm, Lafayette consulted his friend about a bill of rights. They had talked on this favorite subject months before, and Jefferson's influence on the Marquis in this connection was probably greater than appears in any formal record. In January, Jefferson had written Madison that everybody in Paris was trying his hand at framing a declaration of rights and had sent two drafts, including one by Lafayette. In July, before presenting a declaration to the Assembly, Lafayette sent another draft to Jefferson, and on this the latter made a few annotations. In listing the imprescriptible rights with which every man is born Lafayette had included "property" and "the care of his honor," and these Jefferson wanted to omit, leaving only "the care of his life, the power to dispose of his person and the fruits of his industry, and of all his faculties, the pursuit of happiness and resistance to oppression."

Honor, as he had noted when reading Montesquieu in his young manhood, was the energetic principle of a limited monarchy. He was content that the form of government in France at present should be a limited monarchy and raised no objections to Lafayette's reference to the sacredness of the King's person. Also, as the friend of liberal nobles, he still had good reason to value the aristocratic virtues. But the term "honor" at this time and place carried an implication of aristocratic privilege, while the document he was reading was supposed to state the rights of all men. Hence, as he must have thought, it should stick to fundamentals and universals.

His reasons for wanting to omit the word "property," no doubt, were much the same as those that led him to use the expression "pursuit of happiness" instead of it in the Declaration of Independence. He was no more disposed to attack property as an institution now than he was then. The term was used in the Declaration of Rights of his own state, which he had distributed so proudly and which was so highly esteemed by the Patriots at this stage; and, despite his own loss of silver candlesticks by theft, he reported with pride several times that summer that the sanctity of property was generally respected by the excited populace. But he still regarded property, like government, as a means to human happiness—not as an end in itself, not a natural and inalienable right in the same sense as the life and liberty of a person. He wanted to keep first things first. . . .

It was the universal quality in the movement which the Patriots were conducting that most appealed to him, and he was always more interested in the direction the Revolution was taking than in the immediate forms it assumed. Hence his friend's proposals for a declaration were wholly in his spirit, whether or not he was responsible for all of them or the precise phraseology of any, just as they were in the spirit of the world of philosophy in which his mind was most at home. "Nature has created men free and equal"; distinctions there might be, but these were permissible only so far as they were "founded upon the general good"— such assertions expressed his deepest conviction. The phraseology of the first article of the famous Declaration of the Rights of Man and the Citizen, to which others besides Lafayette contributed, fitted his thinking even better: "Men are born and remain free and equal in rights. Social distinctions may be based only on common utility." He was now far more tolerant of aristocracy than he had been during his life among the genial planters of Virginia, but the equality which he regarded as basic was not that of economic and social condition. It was equality in rights, the equality of all men before the law. As a practical statesman he had doubted—more than the leaders of the Assembly, in fact—that the time was yet ripe to urge it, but now he was speaking, America was speaking—just as a whole philosophical movement was—through the mouth of his intimate young friend Lafayette.

Here I discontinue my relation of the French Revolution. The minuteness with which I have so far given its details, is disproportioned to the general scale of my narrative. But I have thought it justified by the interest which the whole world must take in this Revolution. As yet, we are but in the first chapter of its history. The appeal to the rights of man, which had been made in the United States, was taken up by France, first of the European nations. From her, the spirit has spread over those of the South. The tyrants of the North have allied indeed against it; but it is irresistible. Their opposition will only multiply its millions of human victims, their own satellites will catch it, and the condition of man through the civilized world, will be finally and greatly ameliorated. This is a wonderful instance of great events from small causes. So inscrutable is the arrangement of causes and consequences in this world, that a two-penny duty on tea, unjustly imposed in a sequestered part of it, changes the conditions of all its inhabitants.

Thomas Jefferson, from his Autobiography

Marie Joseph Paul Yves Roch Gilbert du Motier, the Marquis de Lafayette, was a French statesman and officer who joined the colonial forces during the American Revolution. During that service he became friends with both George Washington and Thomas Jefferson. When Jefferson was in Paris in the months before the French Revolution, his friendship with Lafayette gave him a contact in the inner circle of the Paris revolutionaries, and it was through Lafayette that Jefferson had the opportunity to read and comment upon the French Declaration of the Rights of Man. Engraving of Lafayette, National Portrait Gallery, Smithsonian/Art Resource, NY.

SECRETARY OF STATE AND PARTY LEADER

FROM "THOMAS JEFFERSON AND THE DEMOCRATIC EXPERIENCE," BY MICHAEL LIENESCH

Alexander Hamilton was a lawyer and a statesman who had served as George Washington's secretary and aide-de-camp during the Revolution. He was a long-time member of the Continental Congress and a strong supporter of the Constitution during its drafting and ratification process. His fervent belief in the necessity of a strong central government and his work to establish a national fiscal system led him into conflict with Jefferson, who was wary of too much centralized power. Hamilton was mortally wounded in July of 1804 during a duel with Aaron Burr. Portrait of Hamilton by John Trumbull, National Portrait Gallery, Smithsonian Institution/Art Resource, NY.

Jefferson returned to America from Paris in the fall of 1789. He intended to return to France after refamiliarizing his daughters with their native country and seeing to affairs at Monticello, but in November, newly elected President George Washington called upon him to become his secretary of state. Jefferson hesitated, but upon the insistence of his good friend Washington, and in the name of service to his country, he accepted the appointment. Jefferson arrived in New York to begin his term in March of 1790. As he had in the governor's office, he was to find his time in Washington's cabinet frustrating and disillusioning.

I n taking up his new position as Secretary of State, Jefferson brought with him a set of strongly held assumptions about public service. As a believer in the commonwealth principles of the British "country," or oppositionist, tradition, he assumed that politics consisted of a struggle between the people and the placemen, meaning the court politicians who were constantly conspiring to create parties of privilege that would subvert the liberty of the people. Furthermore, as the product of an eighteenth-century political culture, he saw the political world as consensual, deferential, and elitist, believing that citizens would choose, as a matter of course, to defer to legitimate republican leaders, men of talent and social standing who would protect the people from these parties of privilege. It was in these terms that Jefferson conceived of himself as a self-sacrificing servant committed to putting the interest of the people above that of any party or person. Arriving in New York, he sought to put theory into practice, calling on old colleagues and friends for advice and counsel and attempting to attract to the new government a set of virtuous and disinterested public servants. . . .

Almost at once, Jefferson became aware that American politics in the 1790s were not to be so simple. Throughout the last session of the first Congress, which extended from December into the early months of 1791, Hamilton and his allies had been pressing, mostly successfully, for passage of a national economic policy. While Jefferson had supported parts of the program and had been active in bringing about the compromise that secured the assumption of state debts, he was deeply disturbed by proposals to create a national bank and a system of excise taxes that were particularly unpopular in the South and West. Moreover, as protests over Hamilton's programs appeared in Philadelphia, arriving especially from the South, he began to express concern about the state of political opinion beyond the halls of Congress. "There is a vast mass of discontent gathered in the South," he wrote to Robert R. Livingston in early February, "and how and when it will break God knows. I look forward to it with some anxiety."

Looking for some sense of political opinion in the states, Jefferson began to reach out. These early efforts can be seen as attempts to create alliances that would later coalesce into a more coherent political party. It was, for example, at this time that he and Madison undertook an extended trip to New York and parts of New England, during which they collected botanical specimens and took political soundings. The political significance of the trip is debatable, but Jefferson's letters during this time reveal his intention of reaching beyond Congress and the new government in search of a broader political opinion. Thus he wrote to friends with increasing frequency during the early months of 1791. In all of the letters, he addressed his correspondents in traditional republican terms, confiding to them as friends and fellow gentlemen, and assuming without question that their views represented not only those of other people of rank and status, but also those of the citizens who looked to them for leadership. At the same time, he seemed increasingly interested in the perspectives of a wider public. . . . The letters show a change in Jefferson's conception of parties; assuming a growing gap between government and the people, he sought to bridge it by bringing the decisions of a distant government before the bar of public opinion in the states. As Jefferson told [George] Mason, "Whether these measures be right or wrong, abstractedly, more attention should be paid to the general opinion." . . .

Jefferson had become disillusioned. Throughout the fall of 1792, stung by Hamilton's charges [that Jefferson supported a partisan, anti-Hamilton newspaper] and smarting at the president's admonitions, he continued to be troubled, as if trying to convince himself that he had done nothing to warrant the claims that he was acting as a party politician. Reiterating his opposition to party politics, he wrote to his friend Charles Clay, refusing to endorse his candidacy for Congress: "Your favor of Aug. 8. came duly to hand, and I should with pleasure have done what you therein desired, as I ever should what would serve or oblige you: but from a very early period of my life I determined never to intermeddle with elections of the people, and have invariably adhered to this determination." Jefferson was far from convincing. Instead of standing on principle—and stopping when he was ahead—he went on to make the implausible claim that he had little political influence. He wrote, "In my own county, where there have been so many elections in which my inclinations were enlisted, I yet never interfered. I could the less do it in the present instance, to a people so very distant from me, utterly unknown to me, and to whom I also am unknown: and above all, I a stranger, to presume to recommend one who is well known to them. They could not but put this question to me 'who are you pray?'" . . .

Jefferson had become what he had before consistently denied, a party politician. All that he believed as a matter of political principle, including every inch of his country ideology, led him to despise the role that he was now playing. Holding his tongue, relying heavily on Madison and Monroe, standing aside while an army of surrogates carried their common cause into the newspapers, he had become nonetheless a leader of the Republican party. Apparently he did not relish the task and seemed sometimes overwhelmed by it. Thus, still at Monticello in September, he wrote to John Syme, "The difficulty is no longer to find candidates for the offices, but offices for the candidates." When he returned to Philadelphia in the fall the situation seemed even worse, and he complained how old friends, now partisan enemies, crossed the street to avoid one another. "Party animosities here have raised a wall of separation," he observed, "between those who differ in political sentiments." Looking back longingly to Monticello, trying to keep his promise to himself to resign his position as Secretary of State in the spring, he felt trapped, unable to leave under the cloud of Hamilton's charges, unwilling to give up the government to Hamilton's increasing influence. Again ironically, and almost in spite of himself, Jefferson the country ideologue, ardent enemy of factions, found himself playing the unlikely role of Jefferson the party politician, leader of a political party formed largely in his image.

These, my dear, friend, are my sentiments by which you will see I was right in saying I am neither federalist nor anti-federalist; that I am of neither party, nor yet a trimmer between parties. These, my opinions, I wrote within a few hours after I had read the Constitution, to one or two friends in America. I had not then read one single word printed on the subject. I never had an opinion in politics or religion, which I was afraid to own. A costive reserve on these subjects may have procured me more esteem from some people, but less from myself. My great wish is, to go on in a strict but silence performance of my duty; to avoid attracting notice, and to keep my name out of newspapers, because I find the pain of a little censure, even when it is unfounded, is more acute than the pleasure of much praise. The attaching circumstance of my present office, is, that I can do its duties unseen by those for whom they are done.

Thomas Jefferson, from a letter to Francis Hopkinson, Paris, March 13, 1789

Jefferson and Hamilton

from *Jefferson and the Rights of Man*, by Dumas Malone

1793

Letters from an American Farmer is published in the U.S. by J. Hector St. John de Crèvecoeur.

1793

TJ resigns his post as secretary of state in December and plans his return to Monticello.

1794

TJ begins planning a major renovation and rebuilding project at Monticello.

1794

The Eleventh Amendment is passed to limit the powers of the federal courts.

1794

George Washington signs the Jay Treaty with Great Britain.

1796

President Washington gives his farewell address, refusing to run for a third term in office.

1796

John Adams is elected the second U.S. president; TJ is chosen as vice president.

1797

French officials, who are referred to only as "X, Y, and Z" in government documents, solicit bribes from American diplomats. Angry Americans cry, "Millions for defense, but not one cent for tribute!" The event becomes known as the XYZ Affair.

I have sworn upon the altar of God, eternal hostility against every form of tyranny over the mind of man.

Thomas Jefferson, from a letter to Dr. Benjamin Rush, September 23, 1800

Jefferson's objectives as secretary of state were to lessen American dependence upon commerce with Great Britain and to expand American trade throughout Europe. He also wanted to keep the United States neutral during European conflicts. His fellow cabinet member, Secretary of the Treasury Alexander Hamilton, had nearly opposite objectives. Hamilton sought to increase American ties to Great Britain, and he was hostile to the revolution in France, an ideological favorite of Jefferson. In retrospect, conflict between the two men seems inevitable, but Jefferson entered into his duties with characteristic optimism.

The bitter political conflict which developed during the presidency of George Washington has often been viewed as a duel, or succession of duels, between Thomas Jefferson and Alexander Hamilton. This oversimplification of a series of complicated situations may be attributed in part to the proneness of almost everybody to personalize political controversies, and, even more, to the general realization that these two men have become symbols of a conflict of ideas which runs through the whole of American national history. No other American statesman has personified national power and the rule of the favored few so well as Hamilton, and no other has glorified self-government and the freedom of the individual to such a degree as Jefferson.

When antagonism is so fundamental, an ultimate personal clash may be regarded as practically inevitable, but no one can fit the events of the first presidential administration into the simple pattern of a political contest between the first Secretary of State and the first Secretary of the Treasury without disregarding other important circumstances and belittling other important men. . . .

Apparently, these two historic antagonists had not met before they became colleagues in the spring of 1790. Jefferson, the elder by fourteen years, was the better known, and various later comments lead to the belief that he was highly respected by Hamilton at the outset. It seems unlikely that he himself knew much about the temperament of his associate. . . .

The military reputation of his colleague probably neither impressed nor alarmed him at first, and he may have been slow to realize how much Colonel Hamilton loved command for its own sake, how little he cared for the liberal ideas of the Enlightenment. Once, when the heads of department met at Jefferson's house, after he had received his things from France, Hamilton saw there his portraits of Sir Francis Bacon, Sir Isaac Newton, and John Locke, and asked him who these men were. They were his "trinity of the three greatest men the world had ever produced," Jefferson said, but they meant little or nothing in Hamilton's philosophy. "The greatest man that ever lived," said the Colonel, "was Julius Caesar."

Jefferson afterwards reported this saying, not as an illustration of the differences between him and his famous rival in matters of personal taste and intellectual interest, but as revealing Hamilton's political principles. He was an honest man, but as a statesman he believed in "the necessity of either force or corruption to govern men." This is the conclusion that Jefferson finally arrived at, but it does not represent his judgement at the outset of his career as secretary of state. He knew that Hamilton had collaborated with Madison in writing the *Federalist,* and he approved that work as a whole, even though he was disposed to attribute to Madison what he liked best in it. How much he knew at this stage about the position Hamilton took in the Federal Convention is uncertain. If he had opportunity during his first weeks in New York to go over Madison's notes on the secret proceedings of the Convention, he could hardly have failed to conclude that Hamilton at that time (1787) was practically a monarchist in spirit, that he had no confidence in popular self-government, that he relied on the interest of the moneyed classes to cement the Union and support the government.

Most of his early knowledge of Hamilton's political philosophy, however, he probably gained from conversation with Madison during these first weeks, and of this, unfortunately, there is no record. Judging from Madison's actions, it is a fair supposition that he did not yet believe that Hamilton as secretary of the treasury was trying to bring about the sort of national consolidation he had vainly advocated in the Federal Convention; and even if Madison had begun to suspect it he might well have hesitated to tell Jefferson so at first. He had gone to great pains to win over his friend to the sort of federalism, with its checks and balances, which, as he presumed, had prevailed. His dispute with Hamilton until this time had been over means rather than ends, and it had centered in financial questions. Not until another winter was the constitutional issue strongly pressed.

One brilliant writer, who has dramatized this period with extraordinary effectiveness, speaks of the arrival in New York of Jefferson's lumbering stagecoach as "an event of tremendous import." So it appears when historians look backward, but Jefferson did not unsheathe his sword as soon as he stepped off his lumbering stagecoach. On the contrary, he entered with good will into a governmental organization which was already a going concern, devoting himself almost exclusively to his own lagging department at first and showing the utmost loyalty to his Chief, the President.

He had been unwilling to accept any political label while in distant France, but he had definitely repudiated that of "antifederalist," and it may have been a relief to him that the state of the roads had prevented him from visiting George Mason at Gunston Hall on his way northward to assume office. To that true friend of the rights and liberties of mankind, who continued to be fearful of the powers of the new government, he wrote after a time that he approved it in the mass, though desiring amendments beyond those already proposed in order to fix it more surely on a republican basis. He did not specify just what these were, and certainly he was not sighing for the good old days of the Confederation, but probably he was still troubled by the perpetual re-eligibility of the President. "I have great hopes that, pressing forward with constancy to these amendments, they will be obtained before the want of them will do any harm," he said. "To secure the ground we gain, and gain what more we can, is I think the wisest course. I think much has been gained by the late constitution; for the former one was terminating in anarchy, as necessarily consequent to inefficiency." He was in an optimistic and constructive frame of mind, and shared George Washington's deep desire that the new government, and especially its executive branch, should be genuinely effective. That was a good reason for co-operating with the Secretary of the Treasury.

This morning . . . I had the following conversation with the President. He opened it by expressing his regret at the resolution in which I appeared so fixed, . . . of retiring from public affairs. He said that he should be extremely sorry . . . and that he could not see where he should find another character to fill my office. . . . He then expressed his concern at the difference . . . between the Secretary of the Treasury and myself. . . . He thought it important to preserve the check of my opinions in the Administration, in order to keep things in their proper channel and prevent them from going too far. That as to the idea of transforming this government into a monarchy, he did not believe there were ten men in the United States whose opinions were worth attention who entertained such a thought.

I told him there were many more than he imagined . . . ; that the Secretary of the Treasury was one of these. That I had heard him say that this Constitution was a shilly-shally thing, of mere milk and water, which could not last, and was only good as a step to something better. That when we reflected that he had endeavored in the Convention to make an English constitution of it, and when failing in that, we saw all his measures tending to bring it to the same thing, it was natural for us to be jealous; and particularly when we saw that these measures had established corruption in the legislature, where there was a squadron devoted to the nod of the Treasury, doing whatever he had directed, and ready to do what he should direct. . . .

. . . He touched on the merits of the funding system, observed there was a difference of opinion about it, some thinking it very bad, others very good; that experience was the only criterion of right which he knew, and this alone would decide which opinion was right. That for himself, he had seen our affairs desperate and our credit lost, and that this was in a sudden and extraordinary degree raised to the highest pitch. I told him, all that was ever necessary to establish our credit was an efficient government and an honest one, declaring it would sacredly pay our debts, laying taxes for this purpose, and applying them to it. I avoided going further into the subject. He finished by another exhortation to me not to decide too positively on retirement, and here we were called to breakfast.

Thomas Jefferson, October 1792

MONTICELLO INTERLUDE

FROM *THOMAS JEFFERSON AND THE NEW NATION*, BY MERRILL D. PETERSON

Having had the honor of communicating to you [President Washington] . . . my purpose of retiring from the office of Secretary of State at the end of the month of September, you were pleased, for particular reasons, to wish its postponement to the close of the year. That term being now arrived, and my propensities to retirement becoming daily more and more irresistible, I now take the liberty of resigning the office into your hands. . . . I carry into my retirement a lively sense of your goodness, and shall continue gratefully to remember it.

I have now been in the public service four and twenty years. . . . I have served my tour. . . . There has been a time when . . . perhaps the esteem of the world was of higher value in my eye than everything in it. But age, experience, and reflection, preserving to that only its due value, have set a higher on tranquillity. The motion of my blood no longer keeps time with the tumult of the world. It leads me to seek happiness in the lap and love of my family, in the society of my neighbors and my books, in the wholesome occupations of my farm and my affairs, in an interest or affection in every bud that opens, in every breath that blows around me, in an entire freedom of rest, of motion, of thought, owing account to myself alone of my hours and actions.

Thomas Jefferson, from a letter to George Washington, December 31, 1793

After the difficulties during his term as secretary of state, Jefferson left the public stage and attempted yet again to retire to private life. But his long-hoped-for return to Monticello, although it did enable him to begin a major renovation project, was to last only two brief years before duty called once more and Jefferson stepped back into public service.

In his mind's eye, Monticello had long been the scene of a pastoral idyl that only now, in the ripeness of his years, took full possession of Thomas Jefferson. Successive calls of public duty had carried him far from his element and robbed him of selfhood. Too long had he lived in what he hated; too long had he neglected the things he loved—his farm and family and books. Return to the orange-red highlands of his native Albemarle—"the Eden of the United States"—was a return to the paradise of his soul.

In letters to friends he depicted himself as a plain farmer, an "antediluvian patriarch" among his children, and a political innocent who, with Montaigne, had found "ignorance the softest pillow on which a man can rest his head." He was still capable of outraged ejaculations on the conspiracy of kings, nobles, and priests against European liberty. "I am still warm whenever I think of these scoundrels," he said, "though I do it as seldom as I can, preferring infinitely to contemplate the tranquil growth of my lucerne and potatoes. I have so completely withdrawn myself from these spectacles of usurpation and misrule, that I do not take a single newspaper, nor read one a month; and I feel infinitely the happier for it." For years he had been accustomed to writing a dozen letters a day; now weeks passed without setting pen to paper as, farmer-like, he put off letters 'til a rainy day. "My next reformation," he said, "will be to allow neither pen, ink, nor paper to be kept on the farm. When I have accomplished this I shall be in a fair way to indemnifying myself for the drudgery in which I have passed my life."

Jefferson was now fifty years of age. His hair was turning gray, but his body was as strong and trim, his countenance as mild, his mind as nimble as in his youth. After a bout with rheumatism in the fall of 1794, he imagined for a time that age had caught up with him. But the torment passed. His habits bordered on the ascetic. He rose early: the sun never caught him in bed was his boast. He neither smoked nor drank, except light wines at dinner and a single glass of water a day. He ate moderately, giving vegetables the first place in his diet. Always busy, "a miser of his time," he expected the same diligence of others, and partly for this reason would not permit games of cards under his roof. He took his own amusement on horseback, riding solitary an hour or two every day regardless of the weather. . . . From the first breath of spring to the last gasp of autumn he spent most of his waking hours in the open air, inspecting his ground and shops and riding over his farms. "I live on my horse from an early breakfast to a late dinner, and very often after that until dark," he said. His ruddy skin flaked and freckled under the Virginia sun. He dressed plainly, put on no airs, and in every outer aspect was the image of the Virginia farmer he professed to be. . . .

. . . Monticello was in noble disarray. Jefferson was tearing down his house in order to make a better one, and the visitor had to keep a lookout for flying bricks. "Monticello, according to its first plan, was infinitely superior to all other houses in America, in point of taste and convenience; but at that time Mr. Jefferson had studied taste and the fine arts only in books," Liancourt [a French revolutionist who visited Monticello] observed. "His travels in Europe have supplied him with models; he has appropriated them to his design; and his new plan . . . will be accomplished before the end of next year, and then his house will certainly deserve to be ranked with the most pleasant mansions of France and England." In fact, whatever its merits, the work of "re-edification" upset Jefferson and his family for quite a number of years. . . .

Jefferson's summit afforded no certain refuge from the political commotions of the world. He said his scheme was to pay no attention to them, but the world would not leave him alone and he had been too long in it to resign himself to the stoical politics he liked to imagine were his. He had been in retirement only eight months when President Washington asked him to serve as a special envoy to Spain. He responded, from his bed of rheumatism, in terms that could not be misunderstood. There were earlier reports that he had actually arrived in Europe to negotiate with one or another of the great powers. The critical state of American foreign relations, together with the Whiskey rebellion and other signposts of discontent on the home front, proved a severe test of Jefferson's political abnegation. The strife of nations and parties broke over the walls he had raised, and before a year passed he was making an experiment to determine the fastest postal route between Philadelphia and Albemarle.

Yet it was a retirement. His principle business of life now was not politics but the management of his estate. "The land left to the care of stewards has suffered as well as the buildings from the long absence of the master," Liancourt observed; "according to the custom of the country, it has been exhausted by successive culture." Jefferson hoped under his own management to make his lands bounteous again; and the outcome of this trial, so long deferred, must decide whether he and his children were to trudge through life mortgaged to British merchants or enjoy the freedom of a great estate. His debts in 1794 were in excess of £7500, and another £1000 would be added the following year by a new judgment against the Wayles' heirs. . . . The goal of debt freedom by the end of 1796 was apparently out of reach. He did not give up on it but was still struggling to reach it years later when he entered the presidency. Under so crushing a burden a man might lose the courage to pursue his vision. Jefferson, however, went ahead with his elaborate plans for Monticello at the same time that he labored to exact a profit from his lands. "I expected when I came home to be quite at my leisure," he wrote in 1796. "On the contrary, I never was so hard run with business." For all the rewards of retirement, it had its disappointments too; and he never found at Monticello the tranquility he sought.

I am going to Virginia. I have at length become able to fix that to the beginning of the new year. I am then to be liberated from the hated occupations of politics and to remain in the bosom of my family, my farm, and my books. I have my house to build [that is, remodeling Monticello], my fields to farm, and to watch for the happiness of those who labor for mine. I have one daughter married to a man of science, sense, virtue, and competence; in whom indeed I have nothing more to wish. They live with me. If the other [Maria] shall be as fortunate, in due process of time I shall imagine myself as blessed as the most blessed of the patriarchs.

Thomas Jefferson, from a letter to Mrs. Angelica Church, November 27, 1793

Jefferson retired to Monticello in January 1794, and despite his long-held desire to be there, he found himself feeling isolated during a particularly harsh winter on his mountain. But with spring came the old passion for the place, and Jefferson devoted himself to a project of renovation and rebuilding that would occupy him for the next two decades. Below, Monticello in springtime. Photo SuperStock.

FROM THE KENTUCKY RESOLUTIONS

THOMAS JEFFERSON

1798

In June, the first of the four Alien and Sedition Acts is adopted by Congress. It requires fourteen years of residence and a declared intention of five years' duration before granting American citizenship.

1798

On June 25, the Alien Act gives the president power to deport any alien deemed dangerous.

1798

On July 6, the Alien Enemies Act allows for the apprehension and deportation of male aliens from countries hostile to American interests; on the 14th, the Sedition Act allows for the arrest of any person who encourages insurrection or publishes false statements about the president, the Congress, or other agents of the U.S. government.

1798

In November, the Kentucky legislature adopts the Kentucky Resolutions, written anonymously by TJ.

1799

George Washington dies at Mount Vernon, Virginia, on December 14, at the age of sixty-seven.

1800

The Library of Congress is established in Washington, D.C.

1800

TJ and Aaron Burr finish in a tie in the presidential election.

1800

The American capital is moved from Philadelphia to Washington, D.C.

1800

Spain cedes the Louisiana Territory to France in the Treaty of San Ildefonso.

1801

After thirty-six ballots, the House of Representatives elects TJ president; Burr becomes vice president.

By 1796, Jefferson's short-lived retirement from public life was over. In that year, once more called to serve, he stood for election and won the post of vice president under the newly elected President John Adams. Jefferson and Adams had long been friends, but as the new government struggled to define itself, they found themselves at odds over the question of how power would be divided between the states and the federal government. Jefferson endorsed strict limitations on the federal branch; Adams believed a powerful center was necessary to hold the Union together. By the end of four years, the two were still serving together, but also running against one another as the heads of the two American political parties. The Kentucky Resolutions, excerpted below, were a powerful statement of Jefferson's beliefs about states' rights. Written anonymously by the vice president, the resolutions were a response to the Alien and Sedition Acts of 1798, which Congress enacted during a wave of international paranoia set off by tense relations with France. Adams intended the acts as a means of controlling foreign influence at home, but in the eyes of the vice president, they were a grievous instance of improper federal authority. The Alien and Sedition Acts polarized American society and set the stage for the election of 1800, in which Jefferson would seek the presidency.

Resolved, that the several states composing the United States of America are not united on the principle of unlimited submission to their general government; but that, by compact, under the style and title of a Constitution for the United States, and of amendments thereto, they constituted a general government for special purposes, delegated to that government certain definite powers, reserving, each state to itself, the residuary mass of right to their own self-government. And that whensoever the general government assumes undelegated powers, its acts are unauthoritative, void, and of no force; that to this compact each state acceded as a state and is an integral party; that this government, created by this compact, was not made the exclusive or final judge of the extent of the powers delegated to itself, since that would have made its discretion, and not the Constitution, the measure of its powers; but that, as in all other cases of compact among parties having no common judge, each party has an equal right to judge for itself, as well as of infractions as of the mode and measure of redress. . . .

In questions of power, then, let no more be said of confidence in man, but bind him down from mischief by the chains of the Constitution. That this commonwealth does therefore call on its co-states for an expression of their sentiments on the acts concerning aliens, and for the punishment of certain crimes herein before specified, plainly declaring whether these acts are or are not authorized by the federal compact. And it doubts not that their sense will be so announced as to prove their attachment to limited government, whether general or particular, and that the rights and liberties of their co-states will be exposed to no dangers by remaining embarked on a common bottom with their own; but they will concur with this commonwealth in considering the said acts as so palpably against the Constitution as to amount to an undisguised declaration, that the compact is not meant to be the measure of the powers of the general government, but that it will proceed in the exercise over these states of all powers whatsoever. That they will view this as seizing the rights of the states, and consolidating them in the hands of the general government with a power assumed to bind the states, not merely in cases made federal but in all cases whatsoever, by laws made, not with their consent but by others against their consent. That this would be to surrender the form of government we have chosen, and live under one deriving its powers from its own will, and not from our authority; and that the co-states, recurring to their natural rights not made federal, will concur in declaring these void and of no force, and will each unite with this commonwealth in requesting their repeal at the next session of Congress.

Our country is too large to have all its affairs directed by a single government. Public servants, at such a distance, and from under the eye of their constituents, must, from the circumstance of distance, be unable to administer and overlook all the details necessary for the good government of their citizens; and the same circumstance, by rendering detection impossible to their constituents, will invite the public agents to corruption, plunder, and waste. And I do verily believe that if the principle were to prevail, of a common law being in force in the United States, . . . it would become the most corrupt government on the earth. You have seen the practices by which the public servants have been able to cover their conduct, or where that could not be done, delusions by which they have varnished it for the eye of their constituents. What an augmentation of the field for jobbing, speculating, plundering, office building, and office hunting would be produced by an assumption of all the state powers into the hands of the general government!

*Thomas Jefferson, from a letter to Gideon Granger,
August 13, 1800*

John Adams had a distinguished record of service in the young American nation. He was a Massachusetts delegate to the Continental Congress, minister to France, envoy to Great Britain, and finally vice president before he became the nation's second president in 1796. But his presidency was troubled from the start. Only days into his administration, Adams came into direct conflict with Jefferson, his vice president, over dealings with France. By the end of the term, president and vice president were running against each other in the election of 1800. Portrait by Gilbert Stuart, National Portrait Gallery, Smithsonian Institution/Art Resource, NY.

THE ELECTION OF 1800

FROM *IN PURSUIT OF REASON*, BY NOBLE E. CUNNINGHAM

"Mr. Adams," said I, "this is no personal contest between you and me. Two systems of principles on the subject of government divide our fellow-citizens into two parties. With one of these you concur, and I with the other. As we have been longer on the public stage than most of those now living, our names happen to be more generally known. One of these parties, therefore, has put your name at its head, the other mine. Were we both to die today, tomorrow two other names would be in the place of ours, without any change in the motion of the machinery. Its motion is from its principle, not from you or myself."

"I believe you are right," said he, "that we are but passive instruments, and should not suffer this matter to affect our personal dispositions."

Thomas Jefferson, describing his conversation with John Adams about the contentious election of 1800

The presidential election of 1800 pitted two old friends and fellow revolutionaries against one another in a contest that defined the great divide in American political opinion. The point of dispute was, quite simply, the proper scope of the federal government. In a campaign letter to Gideon Granger, Jefferson stated that it was his belief that the federal government should be "a few plain duties to be performed by a few servants." Those who supported John Adams believed that only a strong central government could hold the young nation together. The election of 1800 thus became a dramatic contest between two vastly different visions of America's future.

Jefferson's greatest contribution to the campaign of 1800 was in defining the issues before the voters and developing the Republican platform, though that term was not then in use. In letters to friends and party leaders throughout the country Jefferson spelled out his own political principles and what he believed the Republican party stood for. Writing to Elbridge Gerry of Massachusetts early in 1799, the candidate summarized those beliefs, which he affirmed were "unquestionably the principles of the great body of our fellow citizens." He began by declaring his commitment to preserving the Constitution "according to the true sense in which it was adopted by the States" and preventing the "monarchising" of its features. He was "for preserving to the States the powers not yielded by them to the Union" and "not for transferring all the powers of the States to the general government, and all those of that government to the Executive branch." He stressed that he was "for a government rigorously frugal and simple, applying all the possible savings of the public revenue to the discharge of the national debt." Addressing the military buildup following the XYZ affair, he said he opposed a standing army in time of peace and would rely solely on the militia for internal defense until an actual invasion. He favored only such naval force as necessary to protect the coasts and harbors, fearing the expenses of a larger navy and "the eternal wars in which it will implicate us, grind us with public burthens, and sink us under them."

Jefferson emphasized that the United States should stay out of the quarrels of Europe. "I am for free commerce with all nations; political connection with none," he wrote, "and little or no diplomatic establishment." Responding to recent challenges to the First Amendment, the Republican leader affirmed his support for freedom of religion and freedom of the press. No one could have failed to recognize that he had the sedition act in mind when he said that he was "against all violations of the constitution to silence by force and not by reason the complaints or criticisms, just or unjust, of our citizens against the conduct of their agents." Always more than politician, he added that he was "for encouraging the progress of science in all its branches; and not for raising a hue and cry against the sacred name of philosophy."

The Republican candidate expected the views that he expressed in this and other letters to circulate beyond the persons to whom they were addressed, and there is ample evidence that they did so. The principles and issues that he stressed appeared repeatedly in Republican newspapers, broadsides, and party leaflets throughout the campaign. The Republican party took a clear stand on the issues in 1800, and it was Jefferson more than anyone else who articulated the positions that his supporters readily embraced. Jefferson's leadership in directing opposition to the principles and policies of the Federalist administration rather than to the character of President Adams was widely followed but not entirely accepted. Adams again was accused of being a monarchist, though the issue played far less a role in the 1800 campaign than it had in 1796. Adams' policies provided more ample grounds for Republican assaults. Still, some Republicans were less concerned than Jefferson about emphasizing principle. One Virginia Republican argued that there was too much talk of principle and that Republicans should bring their arguments home to the voters' feelings. The Philadelphia *Aurora*, the nation's leading Republican newspaper, declared that under a Federalist president there would be war, but with Jefferson there would be peace. "Therefore the friends of *peace will vote for Jefferson*—the friends of war will vote for *Adams* or for *Pinckney.*"

The revolution of 1800 . . . was as real a revolution in the principles of our government as that of 1776 was in its form; not effected indeed by the sword, as that, but by the rational and peaceable instrument of reform, the suffrage of the people. The nation declared its will by dismissing functionaries of one principle and electing those of another in the two branches, executive and legislature, submitted to their election. Over the judiciary department the Constitution had deprived them of their control.

Thomas Jefferson, from a letter to Spencer Roane,
September 6, 1819

The nation at length passed condemnation on the political principles of the Federalists by refusing to continue Mr. Adams in the presidency. On the day on which we learned . . . the vote of the city of New York, which it was well known would decide the vote of the state, and that, again, the vote of the Union, I called on Mr. Adams on some official business. He was very sensibly affected, and accosted me with these words: "Well, I understand that you are to beat me in this contest, and I will only say that I will be as faithful a subject as any you will have."

Thomas Jefferson, from a letter to Dr. Benjamin Rush,
January 16, 1811

Above, an engraving by John Norman depicts Jefferson as the people's chosen leader. In the center, the Goddess of Liberty holds a portrait of Jefferson while her foot rests firmly on a crown, symbolizing America's rejection of monarchy. Around the goddess's head circle sixteen stars representing the states of the Union; she gazes in admiration at a portrait of George Washington. The portrait was done in celebration of Jefferson's election to the presidency in 1801. Engraving the National Portrait Gallery, Smithsonian Institution/Art Resource, NY.

THE FIRST OBJECT OF MY HEART

THOMAS JEFFERSON, FROM A LETTER TO ELBRIDGE GERRY, JANUARY 26, 1799

1801

John Marshall becomes the first chief justice of the Supreme Court.

1801

The Supreme Court's Marbury v. Madison decision declares an act of Congress unconstitutional and establishes the power of judicial review.

1801

TJ is inaugurated as president of the United States on March 4 in Washington, D.C.; he is the first chief executive to be inaugurated in the new capital city.

1802

The United States Military Academy at West Point, New York, is established by Congress.

1803

The Louisiana Purchase treaty is signed with France.

1804

The Twelfth Amendment declares that the president and vice president will be chosen in separate elections.

1804

Aaron Burr kills Alexander Hamilton in a duel fought over Hamilton's charges that Burr is conspiring a treasonous uprising.

1804

Napoleon crowns himself emperor of France.

1804

TJ is elected to a second term as president; George Clinton becomes vice president in a separate election.

1805

TJ is inaugurated on March 4; he begins his second term as president.

1806

Aaron Burr is arrested and charged with treason for conspiring to create an independent nation in the American Southwest.

In 1800, candidates for president did not campaign in any open or public way—they let their supporters do that for them. But candidates did get their message across through carefully written and circulated letters like the one below, written by Jefferson in 1799.

I do . . . with sincere zeal, wish an inviolable preservation of our present federal Constitution according to the true sense in which it was adopted by the States, that in which it was advocated by its friends, and not that which its enemies apprehended, who therefore became its enemies; and I am opposed to the monarchising its features by the forms of its administration, with a view to conciliate a first transition to a President and Senate for life, and from that to a hereditary tenure of these offices, and thus to worm out the elective principle. I am for preserving to the States the powers not yielded by them to the Union, and to the legislature of the Union its constitutional share in the division of powers; and I am not for transferring all the powers of the States to the General Government, and all those of that government to the executive branch.

I am for a government rigorously frugal and simple, applying all the possible savings of the public revenue to the discharge of the national debt; and not for a multiplication of officers and salaries merely to make partisans, and for increasing, by every device, the public debt, on the principle of its being a public blessing. I am for relying, for internal defence, on our militia solely, till actual invasion, and for such a naval force only as may protect our coasts and harbors from such depredations as we have experienced; and not for a standing army in time of peace which may overawe the public sentiment; nor for a navy, which, by its own expenses and the eternal wars in which it will implicate us, will grind us with public burthens, and sink us under them.

I am for free commerce with all nations; political connection with none; and little or no diplomatic establishment. And I am not for linking ourselves by new treaties with the quarrels of Europe; entering that field of slaughter to preserve their balance, or joining in the confederacy of kings to war against the principles of liberty.

I am for freedom of religion, and against all manoeuvres to bring about a legal ascendancy of one sect over another: for freedom of the press, and against all violations of the Constitution to silence by force and not by reason the complaints or criticisms, just or unjust, of our citizens against the conduct of their agents. And I am for encouraging the progress of science in all its branches; and not for raising a hue and cry against the sacred name of philosophy; for awing the human mind by stories of raw-head and bloody bones to a distrust of its own vision, and to repose implicitly on that of others; to go backwards instead of forwards to look for improvement; to believe that government, religion, morality, and every other science were in the highest perfection in ages of the darkest ignorance, and that nothing can ever be devised more perfect than what was established by our forefathers. . . . The first object of my heart is my own country. In that is embarked my family, my fortune, and my own existence.

I have not one farthing of interest, nor one fibre of attachment out of it, nor a single motive of preference of any one nation to another, but in proportion as they are more or less friendly to us.

THE BUILDING CAMPAIGN

FROM *JEFFERSON AND MONTICELLO,* BY JACK MCLAUGHLIN

When Jefferson assumed the presidency, he had been working on his Monticello home for three decades; still, it was not complete, and would not be for many years to come. As always before in his life, Jefferson answered the call of duty despite a desire to settle in fully to private life at Monticello; yet he also remained devoted to the home and to the project of its rebuilding and renovation.

In February 1801, Jefferson was elected President after a campaign that ended with the electoral college tied at seventy-three votes each for Jefferson and Aaron Burr. This sent the contest to the House of Representatives where it also became deadlocked. After thirty-six ballots, the tie was broken, and on February 17, Jefferson was named third President of the United States. The effect on his building campaign of his election to the presidency was to reduce even further the amount of time he had to personally supervise his workmen. This was mitigated, however, by the fact that his visits to Monticello were made regularly and could be planned for. He wrote to his daughter Maria shortly after his election that he expected to make a short visit of two or three weeks in April to Monticello, "and two months during the sickly season in autumn every year." The sickly season was late summer and early fall, when those who were able to, moved from the coastal regions of the South to healthier climates further inland. The chief danger was malaria, known as intermittent fever, marsh fever, or autumnal fever. It was not yet known that it was transmitted by mosquitoes. Washington, which became the nation's capital in June 1800, was considered particularly unhealthy because it was situated on a swamp. Congress closed shop from August to October, allowing Jefferson regular fall visits to his mountaintop. In spite of the unhealthy climate of Washington, Jefferson was pleased by the capital's being moved from Philadelphia, for it brought him closer to home and eased the burden of travel over terrible roads.

As he began a presidency that was to last two terms, the house Jefferson had been putting up and tearing down for more than thirty years was in no more livable condition than it was at the beginning of the American Revolution. Its size had more than doubled, but probably fewer than half of the rooms had plastered walls and many still did not have finished flooring. The dependency wings, which Jefferson and his wife Martha had planned together during the earlier years of their marriage, were just now being started, but in a greatly simplified version. During the first two years of his presidency, however, building moved rapidly because Jefferson now had at least one dependable workman, James Dinsmore, who was capable of supervising construction during his absences. Nevertheless, it would not be until he retired as President that the interior of Monticello would be finished, and many years after that before the exterior of the house looked like the Monticello we know today.

At the time he became president, Jefferson was in the midst of a renovation of Monticello that he had started in 1796, when workers began knocking down walls of the original house to make way for the new, larger house to be built around it. Work would not be completed until 1809. In 1800, a guest remarked that there was so much tearing down and building up going on that Monticello had the look of a house "going to decay." Yet Jefferson was thrilled with his project and devoted to his vision of the way Monticello would some day be. Above, the interior of Jefferson's dome room, which, while it added greatly to the exterior beauty of the house, did little for the interior, as difficult access made it almost unusable. Photo Robert C. Lautman/Monticello.

We Are All Republicans, We Are All Federalists

Thomas Jefferson, from the First Inaugural Address, March 4, 1801

1805

The Corps of Discovery, led by Meriwether Lewis and William Clark, reaches the Pacific Ocean.

1806

Noah Webster publishes his Compendium Dictionary of the English Language.

1807

Aaron Burr is acquitted of treason in September.

1807

The Embargo Act, signed by TJ, bans U.S. exports to Britain and France in an attempt to force both nations to respect American neutrality in the Atlantic.

1808

James Madison is elected president on December 7.

1808

Congress outlaws the importation of slaves from Africa.

1808

Napoleon authorizes French ships to seize all American vessels entering French and Italian ports.

1809

Abraham Lincoln is born on February 12.

1809

The Non-Intercourse Act, signed by TJ, closes American ports to British and French ships.

1809

The Embargo Act of 1807 is repealed by Congress.

1809

TJ retires to Monticello.

In a closely contested election, Jefferson emerged victorious to become the third American president. His first inaugural address reached out to all American citizens, even those who had supported his opposition, as he sought to unite the nation after the bitter campaign. Still, the new president held firm to his party's stand for states' rights and against the growth of the federal bureaucracy, and Jefferson offered little in the way of forgiveness or compromise for his most bitter political rivals.

During the contest of opinion through which we have passed, the animation of discussion and of exertions has sometimes worn an aspect which might impose on strangers unused to think freely and to speak and to write what they think; but this being now decided by the voice of the nation, announced according to the rules of the constitution, all will, of course, arrange themselves under the will of the law, and unite in common efforts for the common good. All, too, will bear in mind this sacred principle, that though the will of the majority is in all cases to prevail, that will, to the rightful, must be reasonable; that the minority possess their equal rights, which equal laws must protect, and to violate which would be oppression. Let us, then, fellow citizens, unite with one heart and one mind. Let us restore to social intercourse that harmony and affection without which liberty and even life itself are but dreary things. And let us reflect that having banished from our land that religious intolerance under which mankind so long bled and suffered, we have yet gained little if we countenance a political intolerance as despotic, as wicked, and capable of as bitter and bloody persecutions. During the throes and convulsions of the ancient world, during the agonizing spasms of infuriated man, seeking through blood and slaughter his long-lost liberty, it was not wonderful that the agitations of the billows should reach even this distant and peaceful shore; that this should be more felt and feared by some and less by others; that this should divide opinions as to measures of safety. But every difference of opinion is not a difference of principle. We have called by different names brethren of the same principle. We are all republicans—we are all federalists. If there be any among us who would wish to dissolve this Union or to change its republican form, let them stand undisturbed as monuments of the safety with which error of opinion may be tolerated where reason is left free to combat it. I know, indeed, that some honest men fear that a republican government cannot be strong; that this government is not strong enough. But would the honest patriot, in the full tide of successful experiment, abandon a government which has so far kept us free and firm, on the theoretic and visionary fear that this government, the world's best hope, may by possibility want energy to preserve itself? I trust not. I believe this, on the contrary, the strongest government on earth. I believe it is the only one where every man, at the call of the laws, would fly to the standard of the law, and would meet invasions of the public order as his own personal concern. Sometimes it is said that man cannot be trusted with the government of himself. Can he, then, be trusted with the government of others? Or have we found angels in the forms of kings to govern him? Let history answer this question.

Let us, then, with courage and confidence pursue our own federal and republican principles, our attachment to our union and representative government. Kindly separated by nature and a wide ocean from the exterminating havoc of one quarter of the globe; too high-minded to endure the degradations of the others; possessing a chosen country, with room enough for our descendants to the hundredth and thousandth generation; entertaining a due sense of our equal right to the use of our own faculties, to the acquisitions of our industry, to honor and confidence from our fellow citizens, resulting not from birth but from our actions and their sense of them; enlightened by a benign religion, professed, indeed, and practiced in various forms, yet all of them including honesty, truth, temperance, gratitude, and the love of man; acknowledging and adoring an overruling Providence, which by all its dispensations proves that it delights in the happiness of man here and his greater happiness hereafter; with all these blessings, what more is necessary to make us a happy and prosperous people? Still one thing more, fellow citizens—a wise and frugal government, which shall restrain men from injuring one another, which shall leave them otherwise free to regulate their own pursuits of industry and improvement, and shall not take from the mouth of labor the bread it has earned. This is the sum of good government, and this is necessary to close the circle of our felicities.

UNITED STATES CAPITOL.
WASHINGTON, D.C.

While Jefferson was secretary of state, he had the idea for a contest to select plans for a capitol building in the new capital city of Washington, D.C. Jefferson himself anonymously submitted a plan to the contest, but it was not selected. Nonetheless, he did manage to have a significant influence on the look of the new seat of American government. Jefferson corresponded with the architect chosen to build the new city, Pierre Charles L'Enfant, and made many suggestions. On April 10, 1791, he wrote to L'Enfant, "When it is proposed to prepare plans for the Capitol, I should prefer the adoption of some one of the models of antiquity which have had the approbation of thousands of years; and for the president's house I should prefer the celebrated fronts of modern buildings which have already received the approbation of all good judges." Above, a Currier and Ives depiction of the Capitol. Photo SuperStock.

About to enter, fellow citizens, on the exercise of duties which comprehend everything dear and valuable to you, it is proper that you should understand what I deem the essential principles of our government, and consequently those which ought to shape its administration. I will compress them within the narrowest compass they will bear, stating the general principle, but not all its limitations. Equal and exact justice to all men, of whatever state or persuasion, religious or political; peace, commerce, and honest friendship with all nations—entangling alliances with none; the support of the State governments in all their rights, as the most competent administrations for our domestic concerns and the surest bulwarks against anti-republican tendencies; the preservation of the general government in its whole constitutional vigor, as the sheet anchor of our peace at home and safety abroad; a jealous care of the right of election by the people—a mild and safe corrective of abuses which are lopped by the sword of the revolution where peaceable remedies are unprovided; absolute acquiescence in the decisions of the majority—the vital principle of republics, from which there is no appeal but to force, the vital principle and immediate parent of despotism; a well-disciplined militia—our best reliance in peace and for the first moments of war, till regulars may relieve them; the supremacy of the civil over the military authority; economy in the public expense, that labor may be lightly burdened; the honest payment of our debts and sacred preservation of the public faith; encouragement of agriculture, and of commerce as its handmaid; the diffusion of information and the arraignment of all abuses at the bar of public reason; freedom of religion; freedom of the press; freedom of person under the protection of the *habeas corpus*; and trial by juries impartially selected— these principles form the bright constellation which has gone before us, and guided our steps through an age of revolution and reformation. The wisdom of our sages and the blood of our heroes have been devoted to their attainment. They should be the creed of our political faith— the text of civil instruction—the touchstone by which to try the services of those we trust; and should we wander from them in moments of error or alarm, let us hasten to retrace our steps and to regain the road which alone leads to peace, liberty, and safety.

PRESIDENT JEFFERSON

FROM *IN PURSUIT OF REASON*, BY NOBLE E. CUNNINGHAM

In a man of such dispositions, such tastes, who would recognize the rude, unpolished democrat which foreigners and political enemies described him to be? If his dress was plain, unstudied, and sometimes old-fashioned in its form, it was always of the finest materials; in his personal habits he was fastidiously neat; and if in his manners he was simple, affable, and unceremonious, it was not because he was ignorant of but because he despised the conventional and artificial usages of courts and fashionable life. . . . The same fanciful disposition characterized all his architectural plans and domestic arrangements, and even in the President's house were introduced some of these favorite contrivances, many of them really useful and convenient. Among these there was in his dining room an invention for introducing and removing the dinner without the opening or shutting of doors. A set of circular shelves were so contrived in the wall that on touching a spring they turned into the room loaded with the dishes placed on them by the servants without the wall, and by the same process the removed dishes were conveyed out of the room. When he had any persons dining with him with whom he wished to enjoy a free and unrestricted flow of conversation, the number of persons at table never exceeded four and by each individual was placed a dumbwaiter containing everything necessary for the progress of the dinner from beginning to end so as to make the attendance of servants entirely unnecessary, believing, as he did, that much of the domestic and even public discord was produced by the mutilated and misconstructed repetition of free conversation at dinner tables by these mute but not inattentive listeners.

Margaret Bayard Smith, commenting on Thomas Jefferson at home

In contrast to his stormy tenure as secretary of state and the trials of his vice presidency, Jefferson's years as president were stable and harmonious. As the leader of the Republican party, which controlled both houses of Congress, Jefferson nurtured a close relationship with many congressmen and enjoyed the cooperation of both houses of the legislature. Jefferson also enjoyed harmony in his cabinet, which remained all but intact through the eight years of his administration. As Noble Cunningham describes below, Jefferson brought a unique personal style to the office of president, one free of the pomp and formality favored by his two predecessors.

As president, Jefferson made it clear that that he intended to be in charge of his administration and to take the responsibility for its actions. To do so he stayed remarkably well informed about departmental business and was able to respond knowledgeably to department heads when they brought matters to him. The notion that Jefferson was a philosopher who had no interest in the mundane tasks of administering the government derives from images created by his partisan opponents, not from the historical record. Early in his presidency in a memorandum to all department heads Jefferson asked them to send him a daily packet of letters received, together with drafts of their answers. This did not apply to routine matters, but to all subjects requiring a judgmental response. He said that he expected to be "always in accurate possession of all facts and proceedings in every part of the Union, and to whatsoever department they related." Such procedures required steady application and considerable presidential paperwork.

Part of Jefferson's time-consuming labor resulted from his practice of writing all his own letters and drafting his own state papers, while employing his private secretary more as an aide than as a scribe. In appointing young army lieutenant Meriwether Lewis as his first private secretary, Jefferson told him that he would be "one of my family." Lewis and the secretaries who succeeded him were primarily employed in greeting visitors to the President's House, carrying messages to Congress, communicating occasional confidential communications to members, reporting on congressional proceedings, and in other ways serving as an aide-de-camp. Jefferson's secretary did transcribe his annual messages to Congress from his revised drafts and sometimes copied other papers, but Jefferson did the bulk of his own writing and made copies of his letters and other papers in a letterpress. . . .

Jefferson employed no speech writers. He systematically circulated the draft of his annual messages to Congress to all members of his cabinet for their suggestions for revisions, but he never asked an adviser to prepare the first draft. Although President Washington had on occasion sent a bundle of papers to Hamilton asking him to draft a message to Congress and called on both Madison and Hamilton in drafting the farewell address, Jefferson did nothing similar while president.

Jefferson made the cabinet the principal policy-making mechanism of his presidency. "The ordinary business of every day is done by consultation between the President and the Head of the department alone to which it belongs," he explained in describing his administrative system. "For measures of importance or difficulty, a consultation is held with the Heads of departments, either assembled, or by taking their opinions separately in conversation or in writing." The practice that Jefferson most commonly followed was to assemble his advisers in a cabinet meeting—not on a regularly scheduled basis but whenever needed. The government was small; departmental offices were all located close to the President's House, and the president could quickly assemble his cabinet. He resorted to separate consultations primarily when he anticipated "disagreeable collisions."

There were, in fact, few frictions within Jefferson's cabinet; he looked back at his administration as "an example of harmony in a cabinet of six persons, to which perhaps history has furnished no parallel." . . . As a former member of the first president's cabinet, Jefferson was well aware how deep the divisions had been in Washington's administration, and as vice-president he had watched his predecessor face a cabinet more loyal to Hamilton than to the president. Thus, he had reason to remark on the unity of his own administration. Jefferson never had to worry about loyalty and rarely about turnover in his cabinet. His four principal department heads stayed with him throughout his eight years in office; the only changes were in the office of attorney general.

Jefferson's strong popular support was an important factor in making the cabinet system work, as was his own clear sense of being in command in his administration. While he spoke of his vote counting as one in the cabinet, he knew that was only technically true and doubted that the unanimity in the cabinet would have been the same had each member possessed equal and independent powers. He admitted that "the power of decision in the President left no object for internal dissension." Yet his style of leadership was one of persuasion rather than dictation, and there is ample evidence to show that his advisers felt free to speak their own minds without fear of retribution. They also knew that the president relied on their advice and had no advisers outside the cabinet whom he regularly consulted.

Attention to administrative demands led Jefferson to organize his time carefully. He rose regularly at five in the morning and worked on his paperwork until nine, when he began receiving cabinet officers or others who had business to discuss with the president. Members of Congress were free to drop in without appointments. He commonly scheduled cabinet meetings for noon. At one in the afternoon, Jefferson normally went for a ride on horseback—his principal form of exercise. At three-thirty he had dinner, and sometimes invited a guest to arrive a half hour earlier for a private consultation before dinner.

President Jefferson used the dinner hour as his main social activity and as an important tool of governing. While Congress was in session he held dinner parties three times a week,

President Jefferson interpreted his role in a dramatically different way than had his two predecessors, Washington and Adams, who had both enjoyed the pomp and formality of the office. Jefferson did away with most of these ceremonial trappings. He gave up the carriage and six horses that Washington and Adams had used and instead rode about alone on horseback. Jefferson also put an end to the stiffly formal dinner parties that had been the preferred form of presidential entertainment and established a custom of intimate daily gatherings with a handful of friends, politicians, and dignitaries. Jefferson seemed at ease in the office; and the country, enjoying a period of rapid growth and prosperity during his first term, seemed quite happy with their chief executive. Above, Rembrandt Peale's portrait of Jefferson. The White House Historical Association.

The apartment in which he took most interest was his cabinet; this he had arranged according to his own taste and convenience. It was a spacious room. In the center was a long table, with drawers on each side, in which were deposited not only articles which were appropriate to the place, but a set of carpenter's tools in one and small garden implements in another, from the use of which he derived much amusement. Around the walls were maps, globes, charts, books, etc. In the window recesses were stands for the flowers and plants which it was his delight to attend, and among his roses and geraniums was suspended the cage of his favorite mockingbird, which he cherished with peculiar fondness, not only for its melodious powers, but for its uncommon intelligence and affectionate disposition, of which qualities he gave surprising instances. It was the constant companion of his solitary and studious hours. Whenever he was alone, he opened the cage and let the bird fly about the room. After flitting for awhile from one object to another, it would alight on his table and regale him with its sweetest notes, or perch on his shoulder and take its food from his lips. Often when he retired to his chamber, it would hop up the stairs after him and while he took his siesta, would sit on his couch and pour forth its melodious strains. How he loved this bird! How he loved his flowers! He could not live without something to love, and in the absence of his darling grandchildren, his bird and his flowers became objects of tender care.

Margaret Bayard Smith, commenting on Thomas Jefferson at home

inviting members in small groups (generally about twelve), seating them around an oval table with no place of command or honor, offering them good cuisine and fine wines, and engaging them in conversation. When one member implied this was improper executive influence, Jefferson responded, "I cultivate personal intercourse with the members of the legislature that we may know one another and have opportunities of little explanations of circumstances, which, not understood might produce jealousies and suspicions injurious to the public interest." He also said that he depended heavily on members of Congress to provide him with information from throughout the country and help him to sense public opinion. Early in his administration when he still had hopes of reconciling parties, he did not consider party affiliation in issuing invitations. But as time passed, he tended to invite Federalists and Republicans on different days. A number of guest lists for these dinners survive among the meticulous records that Jefferson maintained, and they show that he invited Republican congressional leaders more frequently than others, but most members received at least one invitation during a session. In keeping with his republican informality, Jefferson used for his invitations a printed form that contained no emblems of the presidential office and began "Th: Jefferson requests" rather than "The President requests."

New York Congressman Samuel L. Mitchill, describing a dinner party in 1802 as "easy and sociable," commented that no toasts were drunk and thought the president's French cook "understands the art of preparing and serving up food, to a nicety." Mitchill was particularly impressed by ice-cream balls enclosed in warm pastry. As a scientist, he also enjoyed the after-dinner conversation, in the course of which Jefferson showed his guests a piece of homemade silk cloth from silk produced in Virginia. Talking about a process of waterproofing cloth developed in Europe, the president brought out a treated coat made in England, gathered a pocket of cloth, and poured water into it to prove that no water seeped through. In late 1804 both Mitchill and Senator William Plumer, dining with the president on different evenings, reported that their host treated his guests to water from the Mississippi River and the famous "mammoth cheese." That giant round of cheese, weighing 1,200 pounds, had been presented to him as a gift from a Baptist congregation in Cheshire, Massachusetts, on his first New Year's Day as president in 1802. In accordance with his rule of accepting no gifts, he paid two hundred dollars for it and was still trying to give it away more than two years later. Plumer judged it "very far from being good." . . .

After dining, guests were free to linger for awhile, and sometimes other members of Congress dropped by to join in the hospitality. But the president expected everyone to be gone by six o'clock, when he then returned to his writing desk. He usually stayed busy with his paperwork until ten, and let it be known that he would accept no evening social invitations.

It was during such after-dinner work sessions that Jefferson, toward the end of his first term, spent several evenings clipping passages from the Gospels of Matthew, Mark, Luke, and John and pasting them onto blank pages to produce, for his own use, "The Philosophy of Jesus." "It was the work of 2 or 3 nights only at Washington, after getting thro' the evening task of reading the letters and papers of the day," he later recalled, though he surely must have spent hours previously deciding what passages to select. It was, in fact, a subject of great interest to him and one to which he would later return to compile a similar but more extensive work entitled "The Life and Morals of Jesus." . . .

Most of President Jefferson's evenings were devoted to less philosophical enterprises.

Though this project had been forming in his mind since the issue of his religion was raised in the campaign of 1800, it had to wait until 1804, while he spent long evenings poring over letters of recommendation for office, drafts of congressional bills, foreign dispatches, and all matter of problems brought to him by his department heads. Yet, even during such busy times of his presidency, Jefferson continued a wide correspondence that kept alive his many intellectual interests and allowed him momentary escapes from the pressures of political life. The duties of the presidency, however, always commanded his prime attention, and there were few lulls during his eight years in office.

Jefferson brought to the presidency an informality that reduced the ceremonial role of the presidency initiated by Washington and continued by Adams. He ended the levees— formal receptions that Washington and Adams had presided over, and much to the discomfort of foreign diplomats, he abandoned the formal rules of diplomatic etiquette. "When brought together in society, all are perfectly equal, whether foreign or domestic, titled or untitled, in or out of office," he wrote in a memorandum for the members of his administration. Some foreign diplomats were dismayed at the president's style. When Anthony Merry arrived at the executive mansion in full diplomatic uniform to present his credentials as British minister to the United States, he considered himself insulted when Jefferson received him in casual dress, wearing slippers without heels. When invited to dine with the president, Merry was offended when Jefferson offered his arm to Mrs. Madison instead of Mrs. Merry to escort to the dinner table and followed his usual practice of allowing his guests to find seats at the table pell-mell— a practice that Jefferson also recommended to the members of his cabinet. Merry nearly made an international incident out of what he saw as an affront to his nation, but more perceptive diplomats would find that the republican president was very accessible to foreign ministers, who could call informally at his residence and converse directly with the head of state.

Foreign diplomats were not the only persons shocked at the dress of the president. Senator Plumer, on his first call upon the president, was surprised to find that "he was drest, or rather *undrest,* with an old brown coat, red waistcoat, old corduroy small clothes, much soiled—woolen hose—and slippers without heels." But when Plumer was invited to dinner, he found the president "well dressed—a new suit of black—silk hose—shoes—clean linnen [*sic*], and his hair highly powdered." Plumer judged the dinner elegant, the eight kinds of wine very good, and the president, though in low spirits that day, "naturally very social and communicative." From all reports Jefferson dressed for comfort while working in the large, drafty, and still-unfinished President's House, and he considered his personal appearance of less importance than the affairs of state or his hospitality to his guests. Many Federalists thought he was playing a role in trying to appear a man of the people, but his republicanism was far deeper than the manner of his dress.

The location of the new national seat of government pleased Jefferson for many reasons, among them its proximity to Virginia and his beloved Monticello. During his eight years in office, President Jefferson managed frequent visits to Monticello and carried on with his rebuilding. At right, Monticello. Photo Robert C. Lautman/Monticello.

I . . . have made a wee-little book . . . which I call the Philosophy of Jesus; it is a paradigm of his doctrines, made by cutting the texts out of the [New Testament] and arranging them on the pages of a blank book in a certain order of time or subject. The matter which is evidently his . . . is as easily distinguishable as diamonds in a dunghill. The result is an octavo of forty-six pages of pure and unsophisticated doctrines such as were professed and acted on by the unlettered Apostles, the Apostolic Fathers, and the Christians of the first century.

A more beautiful or precious morsel of ethics I have never seen; it is a document in proof that I am a real Christian, that is to say, a disciple of the doctrines of Jesus, very different from the Platonists, who call me infidel and themselves Christians and preachers of the gospel, while they draw all their characteristic dogmas from what its author never said nor saw. . . . If I had time I would add to my little book the Greek, Latin, and French texts in columns side by side. This shall be the work of the ensuing winter [of 1816–1817]. . . . If a history of his life can be added, written with the same view of the subject, the world will . . . at length see the immortal merit of this first of human sages.

Thomas Jefferson, describing his compilation of "The Philosophy of Jesus"

The Louisiana Purchase

Thomas Jefferson, from a letter to Robert Livingston, April 18, 1802

With some Federalists calling for military action to resolve the issue of control of the Louisiana Territory and the port of New Orleans, Jefferson nominated James Monroe as special emissary to France and asked him to negotiate with Napoleon. Monroe arrived in France on April 12, 1803, but had little negotiating to do. On April 30, Napoleon came to his own decision and informed American minister Robert Livingston that he was ready to sell Louisiana. The price agreed to was sixty million francs and the assumption by America of French debts—a total cost of fifteen million American dollars. Napoleon had abandoned his plans for a French empire in North America in order to attend to more pressing matters at home and in Europe; the result for Jefferson was the chance to fulfill his long-held dream of expanding America into the western frontier. Above, a portrait of James Monroe by John Vanderlyn, National Portrait Gallery, Washington, D.C./Art Resource, NY.

In the same year that Jefferson was elected to the presidency, a secret treaty agreed to by Spain and France turned all American eyes toward the Louisiana Territory, land that stretched from the Mississippi River to the Rocky Mountains and from the Canadian border to the line that now defines the northern boundary of Texas. France had originally claimed this land, but had ceded it to Spain after the French and Indian War. In 1800, however, Napoleon, with a master plan in mind that would spread French control throughout the middle of North America, negotiated a secret treaty with Spain returning the territory to France. The implications for the United States were dramatic. In possession of Louisiana, the French would control vital trade routes and establish a powerful presence on the continent. Jefferson, determined to keep Louisiana open to American trade and settlement, sent James Monroe and Robert Livingston to France on a negotiating mission. Jefferson knew he was stretching the limits of his constitutional powers, but, as he explained in the letter excerpted below, he believed this was an exceptional case.

The cession of Louisiana and the Floridas by Spain to France works most sorely on the United States. . . . It completely reverses all the political relations of the United States and will form a new epoch in our political course. Of all nations of any political consideration, France is the one which, hitherto, has offered the fewest points on which we could have any conflict of right and the most points of a communion of interests. From these causes, we have ever looked to her as our natural friend, as one with which we could never have an occasion of difference. Her growth, therefore, we viewed as our own, her misfortunes ours.

There is on the globe one single spot, the possessor of which is our natural and habitual enemy. It is New Orleans, through which the produce of three-eighths of our territory must pass to market, and from its fertility it will ere long yield more than half of our whole produce and contain more than half of our inhabitants. France, placing herself in that door, assumes to us the attitude of defiance. Spain might have retained it quietly for years. Her pacific dispositions, her feeble state, would induce her to increase our facilities there, so that her possession of the place would hardly be felt by us. . . . Not so can it ever be in the hands of France; the impetuosity of her temper, the energy and restlessness of her character, placed in a point of eternal friction with us, and our character, which, though quiet and loving peace and the pursuit of wealth, is highminded, despising wealth in competition with insult or injury, enterprising and energetic as any nation on earth—these circumstances render it impossible that France and the United States can continue long friends when they meet in so irritable a position.

They, as well as we, must be blind if they do not see this; and we must be very improvident if we do not begin to make arrangements on that hypothesis. The day that France takes possession of New Orleans . . . seals the union of two nations, who, in conjunction, can maintain exclusive possession of the ocean. From that moment, we must marry ourselves to the British fleet and nation. We must turn all our attention to a maritime force for which our resources place us on very high ground; and, having formed and connected together a power which may render reinforcement of her settlements here impossible to France, make the first cannon which shall be fired in Europe the signal for the tearing up any settlement she may have made, and for holding the two continents of America in sequestration for the common purposes of the united British and American nations.

This is not a state of things we seek or desire. It is one which this measure, if adopted by France, forces on us as necessarily as any other cause by the laws of nature brings on its necessary effect. . . . In that case, France will have held possession of New Orleans during the interval of a peace, long or short, at the end of which it will be wrested from her. Will this short-lived possession have been an equivalent to her for the transfer of such a weight into the scale if her enemy? . . .

Every eye in the United States is now fixed on this affair of Louisiana. Perhaps nothing since the Revolutionary War has produced more uneasy sensations through the body of the nation. . . . I have thought it not amiss, by way of supplement to the letters of the secretary of state, to write you this private one to impress you with the importance we affix to this transaction.

FOR THE GOOD OF THE COUNTRY
THOMAS JEFFERSON, FROM A LETTER TO JOHN BRECKINRIDGE

On April 30, 1803, Napoleon decided to sell Louisiana to America. Jefferson considered the sale a great victory, but understood also that it raised many questions about constitutionality and the powers of the federal government. The great advocate for limited federal government now found himself in the position of arguing in favor of an action that stretched the power of the central government far beyond what was specifically described in the Constitution. Below, in a letter to John Breckinridge, Jefferson ponders the many question raised by the Louisiana Purchase.

This treaty must, of course, be laid before both houses, because both have important functions to exercise respecting it. They, I presume, will see their duty to their country in ratifying and paying for it so as to secure a good which would otherwise probably be never again in their power. But I suppose they must then appeal to the nation for an additional article to the Constitution, approving and confirming an act which the nation had not previously authorized. The Constitution has made no provision for our holding foreign territory, still less for incorporating foreign nations into our Union. The executive, in seizing the fugitive occurrence which so much advances the good of their country, have done an act beyond the Constitution. The legislature in casting behind them metaphysical subtleties, and risking themselves like faithful servants, must ratify and pay for it and throw themselves on their country for doing for them unauthorized what we know they would have done for themselves had they been in a situation to do it.

In the case of a guardian investing the money of his ward in purchasing an important adjacent territory, and saying to him when of age, I did this for your good; I pretend to no right to bind you; you may disavow me, and I must get out of the scrape as I can; I thought it my duty to risk myself for you. But we shall not be disavowed by the nation, and their act of indemnity will confirm and not weaken the Constitution by more strongly marking out its lines.

The question you propose, whether circumstances do not sometimes occur which make it a duty in officers of high trust to assume authorities beyond the law, is easy of solution in principle, but sometimes embarrassing in practice. A strict observance of the written laws is doubtless one of the high duties of a good citizen, but it is not the highest. The laws of necessity, of self-preservation, of saving our country when in danger, are of higher obligation. To lose our country by a scrupulous adherence to written law, would be to lose the law itself, with life, liberty, property, and all those who are enjoying them with us; thus absurdly sacrificing the end to the means.

Thomas Jefferson, from a letter to J. B. Colvin,
September 20, 1810

THE NORTHWEST PASSAGE

FROM *LEWIS AND CLARK: THE JOURNEY OF THE CORPS OF DISCOVERY*, BY DAYTON DUNCAN

In a letter written in 1807 to his friend Pierre DuPont de Nemours, Jefferson called the Louisiana Purchase a "transaction replete with blessings to unborn millions of men." While undoubtedly true, Jefferson's prediction was a vast understatement. The Louisiana Purchase allowed America to expand from the Atlantic to Pacific, opening the enormous and beautiful western lands to the generations to come. In an October message to Congress in 1803, Jefferson said that "the fertility of the country, its climate and extent, promise in due season important aids to our treasury, an ample provision for our posterity, and a widespread field for the blessings of freedom and equal laws." Above and opposite right, St. Louis's Gateway Arch marks the entrance to the West; the Jefferson National Expansion Memorial pays tribute to the man who made America's westward expansion possible. Photos the Jefferson National Expansion Memorial/National Park Service.

At the time of the Louisiana Purchase, few Americans had traveled west of the Mississippi River, although Jefferson predicted in 1801 that there would come a time when the nation would grow and expand to "cover the whole northern, if not the southern continent." Jefferson was right, of course, although he himself would never see the vast and wild western lands that so captivated his imagination. Still, it was Jefferson, more than any other single man of his era, who made possible the opening of the West to the American people.

When Thomas Jefferson became president in 1801, two out of every three Americans lived within fifty miles of the Atlantic Ocean. Only four roads crossed the Allegheny Mountains. The United States ended at the eastern banks of the Mississippi River.

To the southwest, stretching from Texas to California, lay New Spain. England controlled Canada; its traders were expanding southward into what is now Minnesota and the Dakotas for valuable furs, and its ships were dominating the Pacific Northwest. Russia, with outposts in Alaska, would soon erect a fort on the northern coast of California. And from the Mississippi to the Rocky Mountains was the vast French territory called Louisiana, where Napoleon Bonaparte hoped to reestablish an empire in the New World.

But while many nations dreamed of controlling the West's destiny, they still knew very little about the place itself. Spanish conquistadors had explored the Southwest. French and Spanish fur traders had ventured partway up the Missouri River, and the British had visited the Mandan Indians in what is now North Dakota. Ships from various countries were now plying the northern coast of the Pacific to trade for sea otter pelts, which commanded exorbitant prices in China. Robert Gray, an American sea captain, had discovered and mapped the mouth of the Columbia River in 1792, followed by his English counterpart, George Vancouver. And in 1793 the Scotsman Alexander Mackenzie had crossed Canada by land, and then had urged Great Britain to take over the entire North American fur business by establishing a string of forts and trading posts across the continent.

For those who coveted its fabled treasures, however, the bulk of the West remained an immense blank—a void on their maps and an awesome gap in their knowledge, filled only by rumor and conjecture.

No one was more anxious to change that than the new President, Thomas Jefferson. Though he had never traveled more than fifty miles west of Virginia's Shenandoah Valley, Jefferson had always been fascinated by the West. His personal library at Monticello contained more books about the region than any other library in the world.

Some of them told him that woolly mammoths and other prehistoric mammals still roamed there. Others described erupting volcanoes and a mountain of pure salt, 180 miles long and 45 miles wide. On the basis of his reading, Jefferson believed that Virginia's Blue Ridge Mountains might be the continent's highest and that somewhere in the West was a tribe of blue-eyed Indians who spoke Welsh, descendants of a fabled Prince Madoc who supposedly had settled in the New World three centuries before Columbus.

Above all, like everyone else at the time, Jefferson believed in the Northwest Passage—a river, or a series of rivers connected by a short portage, that would cross the western mountains, make direct trade routes with the Orient easier and more profitable, and unlock the wealth of North America. Whichever nation discovered the Northwest Passage, and then controlled it, Jefferson believed, would control the destiny of the continent.

For more than a century, the Spanish, French, and British had been searching for the Passage. Three times, Jefferson himself tried to organize American expeditions to find it—each time in vain. In 1783 he had attempted to interest George Rogers Clark, the revolutionary war hero, in a privately financed exploration. Nothing came of it. Three years later, as minister to France, Jefferson had met John Ledyard, a Connecticut Yankee who dreamed of achieving fame and wealth by being the first to cross the continent. Ledyard's plan was to go through Russia to Alaska, then walk from the Pacific Coast to the Mississippi, taking with him only two hunting dogs, an Indian peace pipe, and a hatchet to chop firewood. "He is a person of ingenuity and information," Jefferson wrote at the time. "Unfortunately he has too much imagination." Nonetheless, Jefferson lent his name and some money, and Ledyard set out. But the adventure ended abruptly when Catherine the Great had him arrested in Siberia.

As Secretary of State under George Washington, Jefferson and the members of the American Philosophical Society had contracted the French botanist André Michaux in 1793 for an expedition to "seek for and pursue that route which shall form the shortest and most convenient communication between the higher parts of the Missouri and the Pacific Ocean." Only $128.50 was raised (Washington donated $25.00 and Jefferson $12.50), and Michaux never made it past the Ohio River.

Now, as President, Jefferson decided to try once more. In a secret message to Congress to win its support, Jefferson emphasized the potential *commercial* benefits of the expedition. But he told the ambassadors from France, Spain, and England—whose territories would be crossed—that it would be a purely *scientific* expedition. The British and French ambassadors wrote out passports assuring safe conduct. Distrustful of American motives, the Spanish declined, but Jefferson simply ignored their objections.

At last, in early 1803, Jefferson's persistent dream of exploring the West—for the sake of science, commerce, *and* the national interest—seemed about to be fulfilled.

The river Missouri, & the Indians inhabiting it, are not as well known as is rendered desirable. . . . It is, however understood that the country on that river is inhabited by numerous tribes, who furnish great supplies of furs. . . .

An intelligent officer with ten or twelve chosen men . . . might explore the whole line, even to the Western ocean. . . . The appropriation of two thousand five hundred dollars . . . would cover the undertaking.

Thomas Jefferson, January 18, 1803, from a confidential message to the Senate and the House of Representatives concerning a proposed expedition to explore the Northwest Passage

THE OBJECT OF YOUR MISSION
THOMAS JEFFERSON, FROM A LETTER TO MERIWETHER LEWIS

Like Jefferson, Meriwether Lewis was a member of the Albemarle County, Virginia, gentry. Jefferson selected Lewis as his personal secretary during his first years as president and then, in 1803, displayed his great confidence in the young Lewis by selecting him to lead the expedition of the Corps of Discovery into the Louisiana Territory. Lewis, who successfully led his men to the Pacific and back, found very little success or happiness after the trip. Following a short term as governor of Louisiana Territory, Lewis died mysteriously, most likely by suicide, while travelling through Tennessee in 1809. Above, an aquatint of Meriwether Lewis by William Strickland (after Charles Balthazar Julien Févret de Saint-Mémin), National Portrait Gallery, Smithsonian Institution/Art Resource, NY.

In 1803, Jefferson made a secret request to Congress for money to fund an expedition into Louisiana. The expedition was to be led by Jefferson's former personal secretary, Meriwether Lewis. Congress agreed to pay for the trip, and in June 1803, Jefferson wrote Lewis a letter describing his responsibilities as well as the president's hopes for the upcoming journey. The letter leaves no doubt that, while he would remain in Washington, this was Jefferson's mission down to the last detail.

The object of your mission is to explore the Missouri River, and such principal stream of it, as, by its course and communication with the water of the Pacific Ocean may offer the most direct and practicable water communication across this continent, for the purposes of commerce. Beginning at the mouth of the Missouri, you will take observations of latitude and longitude at all remarkable points on the river, and especially at the mouths of rivers, at rapids, at islands, and other places and objects distinguished by such natural marks and characters of a durable kind, as they with certainty may be recognized hereafter. . . . Your observations are to be taken with great pains and accuracy, to be entered distinctly and intelligibly for others as well as yourself to comprehend all the elements necessary, with the aid of the usual tables to fix the latitude and longitude of the places at which they were taken, and are to be rendered to the War Office for the purpose of having the calculations made concurrently by proper persons within the U.S. Several copies of these, as well as of your other notes, should be made at leisure times and be put into the care of the most trustworthy of your attendants, to guard by multiplying them against the accidental losses to which they will be exposed. A further guard would be that one of these copies be written on the paper of the birch, as less liable to injury from damp than common paper.

The commerce which may be carried on with the people inhabiting the line you will pursue renders a knowledge of these people important. You will therefore endeavor to make yourself acquainted, as far as a diligent pursuit of your journey shall admit, with the names of the nations and their numbers; the extent and limits of their possessions; their relations with other tribes or nations; their language, traditions, monuments; their ordinary occupations in agriculture, fishing, hunting, wars, arts, and the implements for these; their food, clothing, and domestic accommodations; the diseases prevalent among them, and the remedies they use; moral and physical circumstance which distinguish them from the tribes they know; peculiarities in their laws, customs and dispositions; and articles of commerce they may need or furnish and to what extent.

And considering the interest which every nation has in extending and strengthening the authority of reason and justice among the people around them, it will be useful to acquire what knowledge you can of the state of morality, religion, and information among them, as it may better enable those who endeavor to civilize and instruct them to adapt their measures to the existing notions and practices of those on whom they are to operate.

Other objects worthy of notice will be: the soil and face of the country, its growth and vegetable productions, especially those not of the U.S.; the animals of the country generally, and especially those not known in the U.S.; the remains and accounts of any which may be deemed rare or extinct; the mineral productions of every kind; but more particularly metals, limestone, pit coal, and saltpeter; salines and mineral waters, noting the temperature of the last and such circumstances as may indicate their character; volcanic appearances; climate as characterized by the thermometer, by the proportion of rainy, cloudy, and clear days, by lightning, hail, snow, ice, by the access and recess of frost, by the winds prevailing at different seasons, the dates at which particular plants put forth or lose their flowers, or leaf, times of appearance of particular birds, reptiles, or insects. . . .

In all your intercourse with the natives, treat them in the most friendly and conciliatory manner which their own conduct will admit; allay all jealousies as to the object of your journey, satisfy them of its innocence; make them acquainted with the position, extent, character, peaceable and commercial dispositions of the U.S., of our wish to be neighborly, friendly, and useful to them, and of our dispositions to a commercial intercourse with them. . . . If a few of their influential chiefs, within practicable distance, wish to visit us, arrange such a visit with them, and furnish them with authority to call on our officers, on their entering the U.S., to have them conveyed to this place. . . . Carry with you some manner of the kinepox [cowpox], inform those of them with whom you may be of its efficacy as a preservative from the smallpox; and instruct and encourage them in the use of it. This may especially be done wherever you may winter.

As it is impossible for us to foresee in what manner you will be received by those people, whether with hospitality or hostility, so it is impossible to prescribe the exact degree of perseverance with which you are to pursue your journey. We value too much the lives of citizens to offer them to probable destruction. Your numbers will be sufficient to secure you against the unauthorized opposition of individuals, or of small parties; but if a superior force, authorized or unauthorized, by nations should be arrayed against your further passage, and inflexibly determined to arrest it, you must decline its further pursuit, and return. In the loss of yourselves, we should lose also the information you will have acquired. By returning safely with that, you may enable us to renew the essay with better calculated means. To your own discretion, therefore, must be left the degree of danger you may risk, and the point at which you should decline, only saying we wish you to err on the side of your safety, and to bring back your party safe, even if it be with less information. . . .

Should you reach the Pacific Ocean, . . . endeavor to learn if there be any port within your reach frequented by the sea vessels of any nation, and to send two of your trusted people back by sea, in such a way as shall appear practicable, with a copy of your notes. And should you be of opinion that the return of your party by the way they went will be eminently dangerous, then ship the whole, and return by sea. . . .

Should you find it safe to return by the way you go, after sending two of your party round by sea, or with your whole party if no conveyance by sea can be found, do so; making such observations on your return as may serve to supply, correct, or confirm those made on your outward journey. In reentering the U.S. and reaching a place of safety, discharge any of your attendants who may desire and deserve it, procuring for them immediate payment of all arrears of pay and clothing which may have incurred since their departure; and assure them that they shall be recommended to the liberality of the legislature for the grant of a soldier's portion of land each, as proposed in my message to Congress; and repair yourself with your papers to the seat of the government.

In December of 1806, Jefferson told Congress that the Lewis and Clark expedition had been a success. "The expedition of Messrs. Lewis and Clark for exploring the River Missouri and the best communication from that to the Pacific Ocean," he proclaimed, "has had all the success that could have been expected. They traced the Missouri nearly to its source, descended the Columbia to the Pacific Ocean, ascertained with accuracy the geography of that interesting communication across our continent, learned the character of the country, of its commerce and inhabitants; and . . . have by this arduous service deserved well of their country." Although William Clark, pictured above, had been officially second in rank to Meriwether Lewis, Lewis never revealed this fact to their men, and he always insisted that Clark be given equal credit for their accomplishment. Painting of William Clark by George Catlin, National Portrait Gallery, Smithsonian Institution/Art Resource, NY.

A FINAL TERM

THOMAS JEFFERSON, FROM THE SECOND INAUGURAL ADDRESS, MARCH 4, 1805

Never did a prisoner, released from his chains, feel such relief as I shall on shaking off the shackles of power. Nature intended me for the tranquil pursuits of science, by rendering them my supreme delight. But the enormities of the times in which I have lived, have forced me to take a part in resisting them, and to commit myself to the boisterous ocean of political passions. I thank God for the opportunity of retiring from them without censure, and carrying with me the most consoling proofs of public approbation.

Thomas Jefferson, from a letter to Pierre Samuel DuPont de Nemours, March 2, 1809

In his second inaugural address, Jefferson was confident, but still humble; he presented himself as a capable public servant prepared to fulfill his duties. He included in his address a prayer to God for the wisdom and courage to seek peace for the nation. He would need the help as the nation entered periods of troubled relations with France and England, while at home he grappled with the alleged treason of Aaron Burr. Below, in an excerpt from his second inaugural address, Jefferson takes a philosophical look at the coming term.

I shall now enter on the duties to which my fellow citizens have again called me, and shall proceed in the spirit of those principles which they have approved. I fear not that any motives of interest may lead me astray; I am sensible of no passion which could seduce me knowingly from the path of justice; but the weakness of human nature, and the limits of my own understanding, will produce errors of judgment sometimes injurious to your interests. I shall need, therefore, all the indulgence I have heretofore experienced—the want of it will certainly not lessen with increasing years. I shall need, too, the favor of that Being in whose hands we are, who led our Forefathers, as Israel of old, from their native land, and planted them in a country flowing with all the necessaries and comforts of life; who has covered our infancy with his providence, and our riper years with his wisdom and power; and to whose goodness I ask you to join with me in supplications, that he will so enlighten the minds of your servants, guide their councils, and prosper their measures, that whatsoever they do, shall result in your good, and shall secure to you the peace, friendship, and approbation of all nations.

Jefferson's second administration was not quite as harmonious an experience as his first. His relations with Congress became strained while the war between Great Britain and France threatened the peace and security of the American people and called for firm and decisive action. At home, he was greatly disturbed by the machinations of Aaron Burr, a man who had once been his vice president but by 1807 was conspiring to create an independent nation in the American Southwest. Jefferson was troubled by Burr's actions, but found in the affair a cause to celebrate—Burr was unable to rouse the people of the Southwest to join in his treason: proof, to Jefferson, of the strength of the American nation. At left, Jefferson's writing desk at Monticello. Photo Robert C. Lautman/Monticello.

Jefferson's Embargo

Thomas Jefferson, February 1809

The greatest international crisis of Jefferson's second term as president concerned British impressment of American sailors at sea. The trouble grew out of the war between Great Britain and France, which disrupted trade in the Atlantic. Jefferson believed that American ships should be regarded as neutral and left untouched, but the British treated American vessels as hostile and began seizing ships and impressing sailors. Jefferson was hesitant to let America be drawn into the conflict in Europe, but he was equally unwilling to allow such a flagrant degradation of American rights at sea. His solution was an embargo of all trade, meant to force Great Britain to relent. In addition to the political message of the embargo, Jefferson believed it would have the secondary benefit of increasing America's reliance upon home produced goods. The embargo was of questionable effect and was repealed by Congress just as Jefferson was about to leave office; nonetheless, it proved Jefferson's commitment to peace, even as the United States and Great Britain drifted inevitably toward war. Below is an excerpt from the speech of February 1809, in which Jefferson describes his thoughts on the crisis.

The crisis in which [our country] is placed cannot but be unwelcome to those who love peace, yet spurn at a tame submission to wrong. So fortunately remote from the theatre of European contests, and carefully avoiding to implicate ourselves in them, we had a right to hope for an exemption from the calamities which have afflicted the contending nations, and to be permitted unoffendingly to pursue our paths of industry and peace.

But the ocean, which, like the air, is the common birthright of mankind, is arbitrarily wrested from us, and maxims consecrated by time, by usage, and by an universal sense of right, are trampled on by superior force. To give time for this demoralizing tempest to pass over, one measure only remained which might cover our beloved country from its overwhelming fury: an appeal to the deliberate understanding of our fellow citizens in a cessation of all intercourse with the belligerent nations, until it can be resumed under the protection of a returning sense of the moral obligations which constitute law for nations as well as individuals. There can be no question, in a mind truly American, whether it is best to send our citizens and property into certain captivity, and then wage war for their recovery, or to keep them at home, and to turn seriously to that policy which plants the manufacturer and the husbandman side by side, and establishes at the door of every one that exchange of mutual labors and comforts, which we have hitherto sought in distant regions, and under perpetual risk of broils with them.

Burr's conspiracy has been one of the most flagitious of which history will ever furnish an example. He had combined the objects of separating the western States from us, of adding Mexico to them, and of placing himself at their head. But he who could expect to effect such objects by the aid of American citizens, must be perfectly ripe for Bedlam. Yet although there is not a man in the United States who is not satisfied of the depth of his guilt, such are the jealous provisions of our laws in favor of the accused, and against the accuser, that I question if he can be convicted. Out of the forty-eight jurors who are to be summoned, he has the right to choose the twelve who are to try him, and if any one of the twelve refuses to concur in finding him guilty, he escapes. This affair had been a great confirmation in my mind of the innate strength of the form of our government. He had probably induced near a thousand men to engage with him, by making them believe the government connived at it. A proclamation alone, by undeceiving them, so completely disarmed him, that he had not above thirty men left, ready to go all lengths with him.

Thomas Jefferson, from a letter to Pierre Samuel DuPont de Nemours, July 14, 1807, describing the trouble with Aaron Burr

THE SAGE OF MONTICELLO
1809–1826

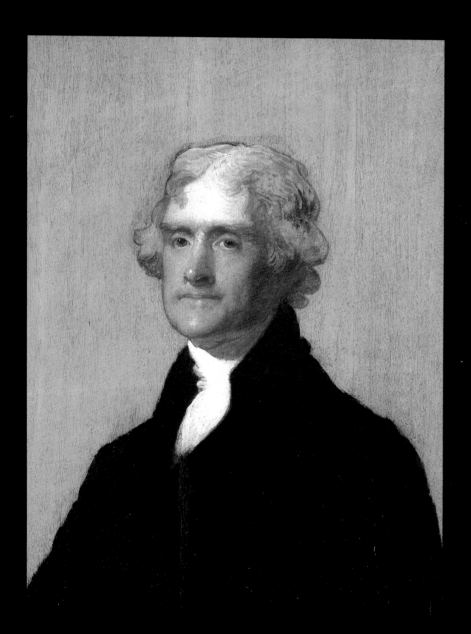

Retirement, when it finally came, found Thomas Jefferson exactly where he had always hoped he would be—atop his mountain at Monticello. In his final years, as he continued the lifelong project of building and renovating his home, Jefferson also struggled to revive the farming operations that had suffered during his repeated absences, and he tried to savor the peace of the place that he had loved so dearly for so many years. But neither his retirement nor his peace was complete. Troubled by debt, barraged with correspondence and visitors, and still immersed in the politics and public affairs of both the nation and his home state of Virginia, Jefferson was far from a man of leisure. Still, he remained, as his life drew to a close, the same happy optimist whose beliefs in the perfectibility of man and his society had led him to work so devotedly for public good throughout his lifetime. He died on July 4, 1826, in his beloved Monticello, amid the same Virginia hills and rivers that had surrounded him at birth more than eight decades before. It was the fiftieth anniversary of American independence.

At left, Thomas Jefferson, by Gilbert Stuart. National Portrait Gallery, Smithsonian Institution/Art Resource, NY (see acknowledgments). At right, an aerial view of Monticello. Photo R. C. Lautman/Monticello.

THE SAGE OF MONTICELLO

FROM *THOMAS JEFFERSON AND THE NEW NATION*, BY MERRILL D. PETERSON

My present course of life admits less reading than I wish. From breakfast . . . to dinner, I am mostly on horseback, . . . and the few hours I can pass in my cabinet, are devoured by correspondences; not those with my intimate friends, with whom I delight to interchange sentiments, but with others, who, writing to me on concerns of their own in which I have had an agency, or from motives of mere respect and approbation, are entitled to be answered with respect and a return of good will. My hope is that this obstacle to the delights of retirement, will wear away with the oblivion which follows that, and that I may at length be indulged in those studious pursuits, from which nothing but revolutionary duties would ever have called me.

Thomas Jefferson, from a letter to Dr. Benjamin Rush, January 16, 1811

"All my wishes end," Jefferson once wrote, "where I hope my days will end, at Monticello." This hope was fulfilled, and in retirement, Jefferson finally became a permanent resident of Monticello. Admirers came from around the world seeking advice, guidance, and a moment in his presence, and he devoted his time and energy to the management of the estate that had been the work of his lifetime. Still, all was not perfect for Jefferson. Mounting debts put Monticello in jeopardy and threatened the future security of Jefferson's family, casting a permanent shadow over his last years. Nonetheless, optimistic and forward-looking even as his life drew to a close, Jefferson found joy and peace on his mountaintop.

Monticello was not only a home; it was a monument. People came from all over: "People of wealth, fashion, men in office, professional men, military and civil, lawyers, doctors, Protestant clergymen, Catholic priests, members of Congress, foreign ministers, missionaries, Indian agents, tourists, travellers, artists, strangers, friends." Some came as idle curiosity seekers, some as seekers of Delphi, others as pilgrims to Mecca. They came to see the renowned Sage of Monticello, statesman, scientist, philanthropist, whose life was identified with the prodigy of the New World, and whose home was among the most interesting of his creations. The monument was even a kind of museum. Visitors noticed "the strange furniture on its walls." In the entrance hall hung heads of elk, deer, buffalo, and mammoth, Indian curiosities from the Lewis and Clark journey, and a variety of paintings, which overflowed into the parlor—portraits of New World discoverers, of Franklin, Adams, Paine, and other Americans, some native landscapes, several of Trumbull's historical canvases, and many Biblical scenes from European galleries—together with busts of various luminaries, including Ceracchi's of Jefferson and Hamilton, who, it was said, stood opposed on marble pedestals in the great hall.

Among the numerous visitors were many Jefferson enjoyed; as for the rest, he had no heart to turn them away. They came, most of them, to do him honor; hospitality was the custom of the country, and there was no nearby inn to which they could go. So Monticello became a tavern, as the President's House had been. During the summers, when travel commenced from the lowcountry, they came in gangs. Edmund Bacon, the farm manager recalled, "the whole family, with carriage and riding horses and servants; sometimes three or four such gangs at a time." Often the stable, which could take twenty-six horses in addition to the family's stock, was full. Martha put up as many as fifty guests a night on the mountain. Of course, they had to be fed. "I have killed a fine beef, and it will all be eaten in a day or two," Bacon said. More than anything else, he felt that the expense of so much company sank Jefferson's fortune. However that may be, he never complained of the company or the expense, though it was a far cry from the simple, quiet retirement he had imagined. Always on display at Monticello, he escaped two or three times a year to Poplar Forest, ninety miles and two days to the south. Before he left the presidency, as building drew to a close on Monticello, he began to build a house at this plantation, and it became more necessary to him when he retired. This second home and refuge, a lovely brick octagon, occupied him for a dozen years.

In 1810, after a year's retirement, Jefferson described his daily routine to Kosciusko. "My mornings are devoted to correspondence. From breakfast until dinner, I am in my shops, my garden, or on horseback among my farms; from dinner to dark, I give to society and recreation with my neighbors and friends; and from candlelight to an early bed-time, I read." His health was excellent for a man of sixty-seven years. He used spectacles only to read at night, and another decade passed before he lost a tooth. He said he read but a single newspaper, Thomas Ritchie's *Richmond Enquirer*, though he continued to subscribe to Duane's *Aurora* and the *National Intelligencer*. "But I wish at length to indulge myself in more favorite reading, in Tacitus and Horace and the writers of that philosophy which is the old man's consolation and preparation for what is to come." He occasionally read new books and grew fond of the *Edinburgh Review*. But the ancient writers were his favorites. . . . Among his most pleasing occupations was the direction of the studies of youths who came to him for books and learning and inspiration, often settling nearby. Some, like William Cabell Rives, had distinguished careers before them. "I endeavor," Jefferson said, "to keep their attention fixed on the main object of all science, the freedom and happiness of man."

Less pleasing, in time a drudgery against which he revolted, was a mammoth correspondence. In a single year he received over 1200 letters. "They are letters of inquiry, for the most part, always of good will, sometimes from friends whom I esteem, but much oftener from persons whose names are unknown to me, but written kindly and civilly, and to which therefore, civility requires answers." Many went unanswered of necessity, but he wrote literally thousands of letters, on every conceivable subject, some of them masterpieces of the epistolary art, and all with his own hand until the last years of his life. . . .

The Sage of Monticello was many times blessed. Good health, good conscience, benign temperament, indefatigable industry, loving family, pleasant country society, honors of a life well spent—all these and more were his. But for his debts and the perilous state of Virginia agriculture, he said in 1810, his private happiness would be unalloyed. For a decade he remained cheerful about the prospects, only then to discover that his hopes were blasted. It was not a tranquil retirement, a life of study and ease and affection untroubled by the cares of the world, such as had always been his dream for Monticello. Once again he realized how much his private happiness belonged to his public happiness. Every renunciation of interest in affairs of state was followed by ejaculations of deep concern. During forty years in the public service he had accumulated quite an agenda of unfinished business. He could not attend to all of it but certain items, above all education, made an irresistible claim upon him. In his private station, aged and remote from the seats of power, he was still a public man, and in the eyes of many the chief personage in the United States. No one, certainly, embodied so well the history and the hopes of the new nation; and although this dream, too, dimmed for him in the last years of life, he remained its most authentic voice until his death upon the fiftieth anniversary of its birth.

Returning to the scenes of my birth and early life, to the society of those with whom I was raised, and who have been ever dear to me, I receive, fellow citizens and neighbors, with inexpressible pleasure, the cordial welcome you are so good as to give me. Long absent on duties which the history of a wonderful era made incumbent on those called to them, the pomp, the turmoil, the bustle and splendor of office, have drawn but deeper sighs for the tranquil and irresponsible occupations of private life, for the enjoyment of an affectionate intercourse with you, my neighbors and friends, and the endearments of family love, which nature has given us all, as the sweetener of every hour. For these I gladly lay down the distressing burden of power, and seek, with my fellow citizens, repose and safety under the watchful cares, the labors and perplexities of younger and abler minds. The anxieties you express to administer to my happiness, do, of themselves, confer that happiness; and the measure will be complete, if my endeavors to fulfil my duties in the several public stations to which I have been called, I have obtained for me the approbation of my country. The part which I have acted on the theatre of public life, has been before them; and to their sentence I submit it; but the testimony of my native county, of the individuals who have known me in private life, to my conduct in its various duties and relations, is the more grateful, as proceeding from eye witnesses and observers, from triers of the vicinage. Of you, then, my neighbors, I may ask, in the face of the world, "whose ox have I taken, or whom have I defrauded? Whom have I oppressed, or of whose hand have I received a bribe to blind mine eyes therewith?" On your verdict I rest with conscious security. Your wishes for my happiness are received with just sensibility, and I offer sincere prayers for your own welfare and prosperity.

Thomas Jefferson, writing from Monticello to the people of his native Albemarle, Virginia, April 3, 1809

MONUMENT TO A MAN

FROM *JEFFERSON AND MONTICELLO*, BY JACK MCLAUGHLIN

In 1826, with his mounting debts threatening the future security of his home and family, Jefferson decided upon a plan to save his house and provide for his daughter and grandchildren. Land lotteries were not unheard of in Jefferson's day, when prices for land were often so low as to make sales unprofitable. Jefferson applied to the Virginia legislature for special permission to hold such a lottery (permission was usually granted only for public or charitable purposes). The legislature approved Jefferson's lottery, in which he intended to sell all but Monticello and some surrounding acreage, but added the stipulation that the house also be included in the sale: Jefferson would lose his home, although he would be allowed to remain there until his death and his daughter for two years thereafter. The tickets were printed, but the sale never happened; Jefferson died before the lottery could be held. After his death, Jefferson's daughter Martha was forced to sell the entire estate in order to settle the outstanding debts. Above, a ticket from Jefferson's lottery. Photo the Thomas Jefferson Memorial Foundation.

1812

The U.S. frigate Constitution defeats the British Guerriere off the coast of Nova Scotia on August 19.

1812

James Madison is reelected to the presidency on December 2.

1813

The Creek Indian War begins in the American South. Fighting will last two years.

Monticello was the work of a lifetime for Jefferson—a home envisioned in his youth, built and rebuilt throughout his adult life, and relished as his final haven in retirement. Below, in an excerpt from his combined biography of Jefferson and history of Monticello, Jack McLaughlin sees in the lifelong building project evidence of the child in Jefferson.

Most of the "conveniences" at Monticello were . . . attempts to solve the kinds of problems that appear in any domestic establishment. They may not loom large in the great scheme of things, but a daily irritant, unrelieved over a period of time, can interfere more with one's peace of mind than events of national import. It was predictable, for example, that with Jefferson's obsession with organization, he would have devised some system for ordering his clothing. At the foot of his alcove bed he constructed a turntable clothes closet. It was described by Augustus John Foster as "a horse with forty-eight projecting hands on which hung his coats and waistcoats and which he could turn with a long stick, a knick-knack that Jefferson was fond of showing with many other little mechanical inventions." The turntable was one of his favorite mechanical principles. The writing table in his bedroom suite had a revolving top, and the high-backed chair facing it revolved to facilitate getting behind the table. In his final years, when he was afflicted by rheumatic ailments, he added a bench seat to this chair to make a comfortable chaise longue that enabled him to read and write in a semireclining position.

Jefferson's household gadgetry has always presented a problem for his biographers; it did not seem appropriate that the statesman-philosopher-architect-scientist should be expending his time and creative energy on such trivialities. Mrs. Thornton expressed this attitude during her visit to Monticello when she discovered Jefferson "very much engaged and interested in a phaeton which he had constructed after eight years preparation." The carriage had been designed by Jefferson and built at the Monticello joinery shop, and Jefferson, who had very likely done some of the work on it himself, was as excited as a teenager with a new car. "The mind of the p[resident]. of the U.S. ought to have more important occupation[s]," Mrs. Thornton observed tartly.

What has been overlooked about Jefferson's fascination with mechanical contrivances is the element of play involved. How many generations of sons have sat with their fathers to explore the workings of old clocks or broken pieces of machinery in a timeless game of exploration? The purpose of these mechanical excursions is not necessarily to repair clocks or fix machines, but to investigate the world of mechanics—and to share a father-son experience. Jefferson's love of designing, repairing, and tinkering with mechanical devices had something of this boyhood excitement at exploring and mastering the physical world. It was childhood play adapted to an adult world, and may have had its roots in shared experiences with a father who worked with his hands, and whom Jefferson greatly admired. Jefferson made of Monticello a toyshop where the adult "law of convenience"—an arbitrary decision that he did not have to abide by formal rules of architecture or interior design—gave him the liberty to indulge his most boyish enthusiasms. Showing off his ingenious devices to visitors and guests was like the child's twin motivations: pride of accomplishment with an appeal for approval.

Indeed, the entire Monticello building project can be viewed as a form of adult play. "Putting up and pulling down [is] one of my favorite amusements"—the most repeated of Jefferson's comments about Monticello—defines house construction as play. To build a house is serious business; to remodel and reconstruct one for amusement is play. It may seem incongruous for a compulsive personality such as Jefferson to engage in construction as creative play, but it is precisely the obsessive person who requires the spontaneity of play as a counterweight to psychological necessity. Jefferson was full of such seeming contradictions: his outpourings of love and affection for his daughters, his admiration for Ossian and the picturesque garden, his falling in love with Maria Cosway in a backflip of adolescent passion, his sentimentality toward his grandchildren. (It should be noted, however, that these were all controlled releases; only at the death of his wife did he abandon all emotional restraint.) His favorite game was that most intellectual exercise, chess, and his violin playing was mechanical, rather than inspired—"according to the gamut." The "building game" fit these patterns perfectly.

This does not undervalue Jefferson's accomplishments as an architect-builder, or his achievement at Monticello. It merely asserts that, as one writer put it, "because I was once a child, I am always a child." We all retain our capacity for the child's sense of playfulness, no matter how seriously adult we have become—as serious as President of the United States, for example. One of the insights into Thomas Jefferson's career as a builder, then, is that his stately mansion, with its magical mystery tour of architectural legerdemain, was erected in part by a boy.

I am retired to Monticello, where, in the bosom of my family, and surrounded by my books, I enjoy a repose to which I have been long a stranger. My mornings are devoted to correspondence. From breakfast to dinner, I am in my shops, my garden, or on horseback among my farms; from dinner to dark, I give to society and recreation with my neighbors and friends; and from candlelight to early bed-time, I read. My health is perfect, and my strength considerably reinforced by the activity of the course I pursue; perhaps it is as great as usually falls to the lot of near sixty-seven years of age.

I talk of ploughs and harrows, of seeding and harvesting, with my neighbors, and of politics too, if they choose, with as little reserve as the rest of my fellow-citizens, and feel, at length, the blessing of being free to say and do what I please without being responsible for it to any mortal.

No occupation is so delightful to me as the culture of the earth, and no culture comparable to that of the garden. Such a variety of subjects, some one always coming to perfection, the failure of one thing repaired by the success of another, and instead of one harvest a continued one through the year. Under a total want of demand except for our family table, I am still devoted to the garden. But though an old man, I am but a young gardener.

Thomas Jefferson, on his retirement to Monticello

So busy was Monticello with the constant flow of guests seeking a moment in the presence of its architect and owner that Jefferson felt compelled to design and build a second home, a retreat away from his retreat. He called it Poplar Forest. Located ninety miles from Monticello, in Bedford County, Virginia, Poplar Forest began as a home for Jefferson's daughter Maria and her family, but she died before the house was complete. Jefferson went ahead with the work, however, and in 1809 began making regular visits there to escape the commotion and demands of Monticello. The house, currently under restoration, has an octagonal exterior which is echoed within the house by octagonal rooms and fixtures. Jefferson made his last visit to Poplar Forest at the age of eighty. He presented the house and property to Francis Eppes, Maria's only surviving child, as a wedding gift. At left, the octagonal house at Poplar Forest. Photo the Corporation for Jefferson's Poplar Forest.

REUNION WITH AN OLD FRIEND
FROM *IN PURSUIT OF REASON*, BY NOBLE E. CUNNINGHAM

1813

British forces surrender the city of York (now Toronto, Canada) in April to American forces led by Brigadier General Zebulon Pike, who is killed in the battle.

1813

American forces win an important strategic victory in the Battle of Lake Erie in September.

1814

The Creek Indian War ends with General Andrew Jackson's victory at Horseshoe Bend, Alabama.

1814

The British capture Washington, D.C., and set fire to the President's House and the Capitol on August 24.

1814

The U.S. is victorious in the Battle of Lake Champlain in September.

1814

A report on the journey of Lewis and Clark and the Corps of Discovery is published with an introduction by TJ.

1814

The Treaty of Ghent is signed, bringing the War of 1812 to a close.

1815

The Battle of New Orleans is fought on January 8. News of the Treaty of Ghent had not reached the city when General Andrew Jackson led U.S. forces in driving back the British from the city.

1815

News of the Treaty of Ghent reaches New York City on Febrary 11.

1815

The Library of Congress receives TJ's collection of rare and important books to help build its collections after the fires of 1814.

1816

James Monroe is elected president on December 4.

Jefferson met John Adams in 1775 at the Second Continental Congress. The two great leaders shared a passion for revolution, but found themselves at odds philosophically. Jefferson was eternally optimistic, Adams gloomy and pessimistic. While Jefferson believed in the perfectibility of man and his societies, Adams, with his Calvinist background, saw flaws and frailties everywhere. After the contentious election of 1800, the two men did not speak or write for many long years, and it was not until Jefferson's retirement that the old friendship was renewed.

One of the most satisfying moments of Jefferson's years of retirement from politics was the renewal of his once close friendship with John Adams. Strained by the political divisions of the 1790s, the friendship between the two patriots of the Revolution seemed ended forever by the election of 1800. Adams, humiliated by his defeat, returned embittered to Massachusetts, while Jefferson, angered by Adams' "midnight appointments," began his presidency convinced that his predecessor's actions were vengefully designed to impede his administration. Toward the end of Jefferson's first term, Mrs. Adams was moved by the death of his daughter Maria to write to the grieving father to share her affection for Maria, which reached back to Jefferson's ministership in France. Jefferson responded with warmth and took advantage of Abigail's letter of condolence to move to restore the severed bonds of friendship. He said that the only act of John Adams' life that had caused him pain was his making his last appointments to office, which he considered as personally unkind. After unbosoming himself of his resentment of that action, he said that he had forgiven Adams and would carry into private life "an uniform and high measure of respect and good will" for him and a "sincere attachment" for Mrs. Adams. There followed an exchange of letters over the next several months in which Jefferson and Mrs. Adams aired their grievances but failed to reach a common ground of understanding before she closed the correspondence. . . .

Not until after Jefferson left the presidency did another opportunity for rapprochement arise, when Dr. Benjamin Rush of Philadelphia cast himself in the role of mediator. A fellow signer of the Declaration of Independence and friend of both men, he had long been distressed by the estrangement of the two presidents. After Jefferson left office, he wrote to Adams hinting that Jefferson's retirement offered an occasion for the reopening of their correspondence. But Adams rebuffed the overture, and Rush waited over a year before he tried again. He then wrote to Jefferson reminding him of "your early attachment to Mr. Adams, and his to you" and expressing his hope that they might renew their friendship through correspondence. Jefferson responded by sending Rush his exchange of letters with Mrs. Adams to demonstrate that he had "not been wanting either in the desire, or the endeavor to remove this misunderstanding." Declaring that he had "the same good opinion of Mr. Adams which I ever had" and leaving to Rush to decide whether the correspondence with Mrs. Adams warranted his continued efforts, he made it clear that the next move was up to Adams.

While Rush contemplated his failure, an unexpected occurrence gave new life to his efforts. During the summer of 1811 two of Jefferson's Albemarle neighbors, Edward Coles and his brother John, were traveling in New England and had an interview with John Adams. In the course of their conversations Adams talked about the politics of his presidency and his differences with Jefferson and added at one point, "I always loved Jefferson, and still love him." When Jefferson learned of Adams' remarks, he wrote to Rush to say, "This is enough for me. I only needed this knowledge to revive towards him all the affections of the most cordial moments of our lives." Jefferson hoped for some occasion that would provide the opportunity to overcome the awkwardness of resuming their correspondence. Rush wrote immediately to Adams, quoting warm passages from Jefferson's letter and urging him to "receive the olive branch which has thus been offered to you by the hand of a man who still loves you." . . .

Adams wrote to Rush on Christmas Day, 1811, and on New Year's Day he took up his pen to wish Jefferson "many happy New Years" in a short letter signed, "with a long and sincere Esteem your Friend and Servant John Adams." He told Jefferson that he was sending him by post a package containing two pieces of homespun that he thought Jefferson as a friend of domestic manufactures would appreciate. When Adams' letter arrived in Virginia without the accompanying packet, Jefferson was so pleased to receive the letter that he did not wait for the pieces of homespun to arrive before writing Adams a long and warm letter, which he began with a brief essay on domestic manufactures in Virginia. He then went on to reflect on the time when they were "fellow laborers in the same cause" and on the difficulties the nation had faced in the years since independence. "In your day French depredations: in mine English, and the Berlin and Milan decrees: now the English orders of council." But before he got carried away, he reminded himself that he had taken leave of politics and told Adams that he had given up newspapers for Tacitus and Thucydides, for Newton and Euclid, and found himself much happier. He concluded by commenting on his health, his daily routine, and his grandchildren and solicited similar "egotisms" from Adams. When he sent his letter to the post office, he received in return the laggard parcel. When he tore open the wrappings, he found not pieces of cloth but two volumes of *Lectures on Rhetoric and Oratory*, written by John Quincy Adams while a professor at Harvard College. The delighted Virginian immediately sent off a note to Adams saying that "a little more sagacity of conjecture" on his part would have saved Adams from reading a dissertation on real homespun but it gave him another opportunity to assure him of his friendship and respect.

The long-broken ties of friendship were restored. The exchange marked the beginning of one of the most remarkable literary exchanges in American history, as the two former presidents reflected on their past experiences, their political views, their presidencies, and their wide interests. They debated political theory and philosophy, discussed their reading, past and present, and ranged widely over the whole of human experience. Their speculations in political theory and on the nature of man and society left for posterity such fascinating exchanges as their discussion of aristocracy, which drew from Jefferson an essay on natural and artificial aristocracy and the form of government that best provided for the elevation of the "good and wise" into office. The elder statesmen could not free themselves from the realm of politics that had engrossed their lives, but they seemed to derive the most pleasure from discussing historical, scientific, and religious subjects. They exchanged information and opinions on the American Indians and on their own regions. And they bombarded each other with ideas that provoked response. Through the last year of their lives, letters continued to pass between Quincy and Monticello.

The circumstances of the times in which we have happened to live, and the partiality of our friends at a particular period, placed us in a state of apparent opposition, which some might suppose to be personal also; and there might not be wanting those who wished to make it so, by filling our ears with malignant falsehoods, by dressing up hideous phantoms of their own creation, presenting them to you under my name, to me under yours, and endeavoring to instill into our minds things concerning each other the most destitute of truth. And if there had been, at any time, a moment when we were off our guard, and in a temper to let the whispers of these people make us forget what we had known of each other for so many years, and years of so much trial. Yet all men who have attended to the workings of the human mind, who have seen the false colors under which passion sometimes dresses the actions and motives of others, have also seen those passions subsiding with time and reflection, dissipating like mists before the rising sun, and restoring to us the sight of all things in their true shape and colors. It would be strange indeed, if, at our years, we were to go back an age to hunt up imaginary or forgotten facts, to disturb the repose of affections so sweetening to the evening of our lives. Be assured, my dear Sir, that I am incapable of receiving the slightest impression from the effort now made to plant thorns on the pillow of age, worth, and wisdom, and to sow tares between friends who have been such for nearly half a century. Beseeching you then, not to suffer your mind to be disquieted by this wicked attempt to poison its peace, and praying you to throw it among the things which have never happened, I add sincere assurances of my unabated and constant attachment, friendship, and respect.

Thomas Jefferson, from a letter to John Adams, October 12, 1823

FATHER OF A UNIVERSITY

FROM *THOMAS JEFFERSON AND THE NEW NATION*, BY MERRILL D. PETERSON

1817

The First Seminole War begins; fighting in Florida and Georgia will continue for two years.

1817

Construction begins in July on the Erie Canal.

1818

On January 1, a reception is held to celebrate the reopening of the President's House, restored after the fires of 1814. It is now called the White House in honor of its sparkling new coat of paint.

Years before construction began on the University of Virginia, Jefferson wrote to a friend about his idea for a new architectural plan for universities. "It is infinitely better to erect a small and separate building for each separate professorship, . . . joining the lodges by barracks for a certain portion of students. . . . The whole of these arranged around an open square of grass and trees would make it . . . an academical village, instead of a large and common den of noise, of filth, and of fetid air." Eventually, Jefferson brought this dream to life. Below, Jefferson's Rotunda at the University of Virginia, flanked by the twin rows of academic and residential buildings. Photo University of Virginia.

Jefferson considered the establishment of an educational system in the state of Virginia a "holy cause." In his view, a free government required an educated populace. He had long advocated a plan for general education in Virginia from the elementary grades on, but in retirement, he focused on creating a world class university in his native state. He would be the planner, the architect, and the builder of the University of Virginia, as well as the mastermind behind its buildings and grounds, its curriculum, its faculty, and its rules and regulations. Jefferson listed the University as one of his three greatest achievements, along with the Declaration of Independence and the Act for Establishing Religious Freedom in Virginia.

The University of Virginia, chartered in 1819, was as much his personal creation as Monticello, the Declaration of Independence, or the Lewis and Clark expedition. And perhaps nothing contained so well the dominant forces of his life and mind, of democracy and enlightenment and nationality, as his vision of a great university. The vision passed through several phases before it came to realization. Initially, in 1779, Jefferson sought to transform William and Mary into a secular institution of university caliber. He failed in this and gradually lost all hope of reforming his alma mater. In 1794 he felt keen interest in the proposal of a Swiss exile from revolution, Francois d'Invernois, to remove the whole College of Geneva to the United States. When the General Assembly passed up the opportunity, Jefferson recommended it to President Washington in the belief that this seminary, one of the finest in Europe in his opinion, might become the foundation of a national university. But Washington thought the hazards of transplanting a foreign college, and a foreign-speaking faculty, too great. Jefferson himself had earlier warned against one experiment in this line, the establishment of a French academy of arts and sciences in Richmond under the direction of Quesnay de Beaurepaire, which had already failed.

In 1800 he first seriously turned his thoughts to the creation of a wholly new institution in his native state. From his friends Priestly and Dupont he requested the plan of a university "so broad and liberal and modern as to be worth patronizing with public support, and be a temptation to the youth of other states to come and drink of the cup of knowledge and fraternize with us." Priestly offered a series of useful suggestions, while Dupont furnished an elaborate plan of national education. Neither altogether suited Jefferson's purposes. At this stage he aimed at a state university, modestly begun but large in conception, and national in spirit and service and outline. In January 1805 he wrote a four-page prospectus for such a university in reply to the request of Littleton Waller Tazewell, who seemed to believe that the

General Assembly had been brought to the point of action. Already Georgia, North Carolina, South Carolina, and Tennessee had established state universities, and though they existed mostly on paper, Virginia could not be indifferent to the movement. The letter to Tazewell was the genesis of Jefferson's plan for the University of Virginia. Emphasizing the modernity of his conception, he called not only for redefinition of higher education but for a university geared to the constantly advancing knowledge of the times. "Science is progressive," he wrote. "What was useful two centuries ago is now become useless; e.g., one half of the professorships of William and Mary. What is now deemed useful will in some of its parts become useless in another century. . . . Everyone knows that Oxford, Cambridge, the Sorbonne, etc. are now a century or two behind the sciences of the age." Perhaps as an inducement to the legislature, Jefferson offered the legacy of his library to the meditated university. But it was not to be. When Virginia remained mute after the passage of two years, Jefferson set aside his hopes in this direction, and in December 1806 recommended a national university to Congress. . . .

Jefferson had been in retirement for five years before he became associated with the enterprise that led to the establishment of the University of Virginia. Several of his neighbors . . . were endeavoring in 1814 to set up a private secondary school, Albemarle Academy, in Charlottesville. Petty academies of this kind, Jefferson told Adams, dotted the state. "They commit their pupils to the theatre of the world with just taste enough of learning to be alienated from industrious pursuits, and not enough to do service in the ranks of science." Placed on the board of the fledgling academy, he at once set out to escalate it into a college and then a university. In September he drafted a bill to accomplish the first step, the conversion of Albemarle Academy into Central College. The bill failed in the ensuing session of the legislature but passed in February 1816. By the act of incorporation Central College was a private non-sectarian seminary with no other resources than it could raise from the sale of the two glebes in Albemarle (the parish lands of the old Established Church), from voluntary subscriptions, and from lottery. However, the charter provided for a liberal enlargement of the educational plan to reach the objects of a state university and divested the college of its local character by placing the appointment of the Board of Visitors in the governor and making him an ex officio member. . . . In the space of two years a lifeless academy had been transformed into the design of a state university.

Other hopes and plans would also fail, but a dream had become a reality and the founder would not live to trace its tortuous history. Jefferson's labors for the University absorbed him almost until the hour of his death. At the end of April 1826, he laid out the plan of a botanical garden. On his last visit to the grounds, as he watched the raising of the great marble capitals atop the columns of the rotunda, he must have reflected on the agony and the ecstasy of this triumph. "I have long been sensible," he had written three months before, "that while I was endeavoring to render my country the greatest of all services, that of regenerating the public education, and placing the rising generation on the level of our sister states . . . , I was discharging the odious function of a physician pouring medicine down the throat of a patient insensible of needing it." Yet with courage, faith, and skill rarely equalled, he had succeeded—at least with the University. It was his monument. If Emerson's aphorism, "An institution is the lengthened shadow of one man," has any truth, it belongs to Jefferson and the University of Virginia.

from Thomas Jefferson and the New Nation,
by Merrill D. Peterson

Before his death, Jefferson instructed that his final resting place be marked by "the following inscription and not a word more: 'Here was buried Thomas Jefferson, Author of the Declaration of American Independence, of the Statute of Virginia for Religious Freedom, and Father of the University of Virginia.'" At right, Jefferson's gravesite at Monticello. Photo the Thomas Jefferson Memorial Foundation.

A LEGACY OF HOPE

FROM *THE AMERICAN POLITICAL TRADITION*, BY RICHARD HOFSTADTER

1819

A new immigration law establishes rules and procedures for ships carrying immigrants into American harbors.

1820

The Missouri Compromise attempts to maintain the balance between slave and free states in the Union by declaring that slavery will not be legal in states drawn from the Louisiana Purchase territory north of 36°30″N latitude, which is the contemplated southern boundary of Missouri. Missouri itself is the compromise, admitted to the Union as a slave state at the same time Maine enters as a free state.

1820

James Monroe is reelected president on December 6.

1821

The first American settlements are established in Texas.

1823

President Monroe enunciates what will become known as the Monroe Doctrine in his annual message to Congress. He declares that the U.S. will not stand for European intervention in its affairs, nor will America become involved in European quarrels.

1824

Jedediah Strong Smith establishes a gateway though the Rocky Mountains at South Pass.

1824

In presidential elections, no candidate receives an electoral majority; John Quincy Adams is later chosen president by the House of Representatives.

1824

Illinois abolishes slavery.

1826

TJ dies at Monticello on July 4, the fiftieth anniversary of the Declaration of Independence. John Adams dies the same day.

In his final years, Jefferson was troubled by the direction the nation was taking. He was disturbed by the way the Missouri Compromise had polarized the states; he worried about the power of the Supreme Court, and he saw the growing central government as a threat to the freedom of the individual and of the states. But Jefferson remained optimistic, believing as he always had that man had it within him to improve the quality of his life and of his society and that the nation he had helped to found had the most solid and promising foundation of any yet begun. Jefferson died on July 4, 1826, on the fiftieth anniversary of American independence.

And Jefferson himself? He lived through his last years without bitterness or anger, certainly without a sense of defeat. His country, in spite of one short-lived depression, was growing and flourishing, and as he looked down upon it from his mountaintop he predicted hopefully that the process of civilization would continue to sweep across the continent from east to west "like a cloud of light." He busied himself answering his voluminous correspondence, interpreting for inquirers the history of his times, trading opinions with scientists and inventors, trying to steady his failing fortunes, and laying the foundation of the University of Virginia, which gave him special pride. He renewed his old friendship with John Adams, and once again argued with him the case of democracy. At the age of seventy-eight he wrote to the old man at Quincy: "I shall not die without a hope that light and liberty are on steady advance." When Adams asked if he would choose to live his life over again, he replied in the affirmative, at least for the greater part of it. "From twenty-five to sixty, I would say yes: and I might go further back, but not come lower down." "I enjoy good health," he went on, "I am happy in what is around me, yet I assure you I am ripe for leaving all, this year, this day, this hour. Nothing proves more than this that the Being who presides over the world is essentially benevolent."

Here speaks the antithesis of the tragic temperament. Through all of Jefferson's work there runs like a fresh underground stream the deep conviction that all will turn out well, that life will somehow assert itself. Wherever he was, he managed to find it good, and in these last years he never felt the need of moving more than a few miles from Monticello. Life had always come more than halfway to meet him, just as visitors now came from everywhere in the Western World to find him out on his mountaintop. For him no defeat could ever be more than a temporary interruption in the smooth flow of things toward their benevolent end. It was not after all a system of economics or politics that he was leaving, not even a political party, but an imperishable faith expressed in imperishable rhetoric. It did not matter that his agrarianism was in retreat, that his particularism was falling into the hands of proslavery apologists whom he would have detested, that his individualism would become the doctrine of plutocrats and robber barons. His sense of values would survive. Men like Hamilton could argue that manufactures ought to be promoted because they would enable the nation to use the labor of women and children, "many of them at a tender age," but Jefferson was outraged at such a view of humanity. Hamilton schemed to get the children into factories; Jefferson planned school systems. While Hamilton valued institutions and abstractions, Jefferson valued people and found no wealth more important than life. If he had gone astray as to means, he had at least kept his eyes on his original end—the pursuit of happiness.

One of the last survivors among the founders, Jefferson lived to see himself become an object of veneration, and as his life ebbed out he might easily have observed with the dying Roman Emperor: "I feel myself becoming a god." But he had no desire that he and his contemporaries should become oracles to future generations. "The earth," he was fond of saying, "belongs to the living." The world changes, and truth cannot be embalmed.

Some men look at constitutions with sanctimonious reverence, and deem them like the ark of the covenant, too sacred to be touched. They ascribe to the proceeding age a wisdom more than human, and suppose that they did it to be beyond amendment. I knew that age well; I belonged to it and labored with it. It deserved well of its country. It was very like the present, but without the experience of the present; and forty years of experience in government is worth a century of book-reading; and this they would say for themselves, were they to rise from the dead. I am certainly not an advocate for frequent and untried changes in laws and institutions. . . . But I know also, that laws and institutions must go hand in hand with the progress of the human mind. As that becomes more developed, more enlightened, as new discoveries are made, new truths disclosed, and manners and opinions change, with the change of circumstances, institutions must advance also, and keep pace with the times. We might as well require a man to wear still the coat which fitted him when a boy, as civilized society to remain ever under the regime of their barbarious ancestors.

Two years before his death, he wrote: "Nothing then is unchangeable but the inherent and unalienable rights of man."

All eyes are opened, or opening, to the rights of man. The general spread of the light of science has already laid open to every view the palpable truth, that the mass of mankind has not been born with saddles on their backs, nor a favored few booted and spurred, ready to ride them legitimately, by the grace of God. These are the grounds of hope for others. For ourselves, let the annual return of this day forever refresh our recollections of these rights, and an undiminished devotion to them.

Thomas Jefferson, from a letter written ten days before death, declining an invitation to speak at an Independence Day celebration in Washington, D.C.

At the dedication of the Jefferson Memorial in Washington, D.C., President Franklin Roosevelt, a leader in the movement to build the memorial, said, "We dedicate a shrine to freedom. To Thomas Jefferson, Apostle of Freedom." At left, the Jefferson Memorial in springtime. Photo SuperStock.

BIBLIOGRAPHY

Betts, Edwin Morris and James Adam Bear, Jr., editors. *The Family Letters of Thomas Jefferson.* University Press of Virginia, 1986. This book gives the reader a glimpse of Thomas Jefferson as a man devoted to his family and home, as well as to the new country he was so influential in founding.

Colbert, David, editor. *Eyewitness to America: 500 Years of America in the Words of Those Who Saw It Happen.* Pantheon, 1997. This intriguing book is composed of hundreds of first-hand accounts of the events of American history.

Cunningham, Noble E., Jr. *In Pursuit of Reason: The Life of Thomas Jefferson.* Ballantine, 1988. This authoritative biography of Thomas Jefferson offers a comprehensive and insightful overview of Jefferson's life and work.

Duncan, Dayton. *Lewis & Clark.* Alfred A. Knopf, 1997. A companion to the critically acclaimed documentary film by Ken Burns, this book details the journey of the Corps of Discovery.

Hofstadter, Richard. *The American Political Tradition and the Men Who Made It.* Alfred A. Knopf, 1964. This book explores the lives and philosophies of the Founding Fathers.

Koch, Adrienne and William Peden, editors. *The Life and Selected Writings of Thomas Jefferson.* Modern Library, 1993. This volume of Jefferson's most important works and letters gives the reader Thomas Jefferson, in his own words.

Levy, Leonard. *Constitutional Opinions: Aspects of the Bill of Rights.* Oxford University Press, 1986. This book studies the philosophical and legal challenges of the Bill of Rights.

Malone, Dumas. *Jefferson and His Time.* Vol. 1, *Jefferson the Virginian,* 1948; Vol. 2, *Jefferson and the Rights of Man,* 1951. Little, Brown and Company. This definitive work offers an in-depth study of the times and legacy of Thomas Jefferson.

Mayo, Bernard, editor. *Jefferson Himself: The Personal Narrative of a Many-Sided American.* University Press of Virginia, 1970. Mayo has selected passages from various writings of Jefferson to illustrate the importance of Jefferson's contributions.

McLaughlin, Jack. *Jefferson and Monticello: The Biography of a Builder.* Henry Holt, 1990. This book details Jefferson's passion for the building and rebuilding of his home.

Onuf, Peter S., editor. *Jeffersonian Legacies.* University Press of Virginia, 1993. In this book, Onuf brings together the essays of many Jefferson scholars.

Peterson, Merrill. *Thomas Jefferson and the New Nation.* Oxford University Press, 1970. This book is an engaging and informative biography of Thomas Jefferson.

Stein, Susan R. *The Worlds of Thomas Jefferson at Monticello.* Harry N. Abrams, 1993. This beautiful book offers many color photographs and information about the house, grounds, and interior of Jefferson's beloved home, Monticello.

TRACKING THOMAS JEFFERSON

VIRGINIA

Monticello, *Charlottesville, Virginia.* The home that Jefferson worked most of his life to build is now owned and operated by the Thomas Jefferson Memorial Foundation, which purchased the house and land in 1923. Monticello, located in central Virginia, now operates as a museum and educational center and is the only American home on the United Nations' World Heritage List. Next door to Monticello is the International Center for Jefferson Studies at Kenwood. *The Thomas Jefferson Memorial Foundation, P.O. Box 217, Charlottesville, VA 22902.*
(804-984-9822)

The Thomas Jefferson Center for Historic Plants, *at Monticello, Charlottesville, Virginia.* A tribute to Jefferson's interest in horticulture, this center is devoted to the collection, preservation, and distribution of plants from early American gardens. Plants are sold in a garden shop on the premises, and seeds are available through the center's newsletter. *The Thomas Jefferson Center for Historic Plants, P.O. Box 316, Charlottesville, VA 22902.*
(804-984-9822)

Poplar Forest, *near Lynchburg, Virginia.* Located in Bedford County, fifty miles from Monticello, Poplar Forest is the home that Jefferson built late in life as a retreat from the hectic pace of Monticello. The octagonal house is on the register of National Historic Landmarks and is open for guided tours. *Thomas Jefferson's Poplar Forest, P.O. Box 419, Forest, VA 24551.*
(804-525-1806)

The University of Virginia, *Charlottesville, Virginia.* After retiring from public life, Jefferson secured the land, raised the funds, and designed the buildings and grounds for Virginia's state university. He counted the founding of the University of Virginia as one of the three great achievements of his lifetime. Guided tours of the grounds and historic buildings of the university are offered, free of charge.
(804-982-3200)

WASHINGTON, D.C.

The National Archives. Featured in the Rotunda of the Archives is the original copy of the Declaration of Independence, drafted by Thomas Jefferson in 1776. Located at Seventh Street and Pennsylvania Avenue Northwest, the building is open every day except Christmas.
(202-501-5130)

PHILADELPHIA, PENNSYLVANIA

Independence National Historic Site. Jefferson presented the completed draft of the Declaration of Independence to the Continental Congress inside Philadelphia's Independence Hall. This building, and other historic sites in the city, can be visited as part of a tour offered by the National Park Service. *The Philadelphia National Historic Site, 313 Walnut Street, Philadelphia, PA 19106.*
(215-597-8974)

INDEX

Page numbers in *italic* type refer to photographs and illustrations.